Exceeding Righteousness:
Studies in the Sermon on the Mount

Gary C. Redding

Exceeding Righteousness:
Studies in the Sermon on the Mount

Gary C. Redding

Parson's Porch
Books
Cleveland, TN

Parson's Porch Books

Copyright (C) 2011 by Gary C. Redding

ISBN: Softcover   978-1-936912-32-2

This book was printed in the United States of America.

To order additional copies of this book, contact:

Parson's Porch Books
c/o Parson's Porch, Inc
1-423-475-7308
www.parsonsporch.com

Table of Contents

IT'S CLOSER THAN YOU THINK!
Matthew 4:12-17

A LITTLE BOY ASKED HIS MOTHER one day if she knew what Goliath said when David hit him in the head with a stone.

"Well, I didn't know Goliath said anything," she replied.

The little boy nodded his head knowingly and said, "Yep, he sure did. When David put that stone in his slingshot and swung it around and around, and let it go and hit ol' Goliath right between the eyes, Goliath said, 'Hmmmmm, nothing like that has ever entered my mind before.'"

That is the aim of this sermon: to offer some new ideas and insights related to the kingdom of God that have never entered your mind before. Perhaps, I'll also be able to answer some of your questions and dispel some of your confusion about God's kingdom. That's certainly my hope and it's been my prayer in the preparation of the message.

There are several good reasons why we all need a better understanding of the New Testament teaching about the kingdom of God. To begin, both Matthew(4:17) and Mark(1:14) agree that the kingdom was the subject Jesus addressed first, as well as most frequently and consistently during his ministry. It clearly was his all-consuming passion. The kingdom is mentioned no fewer than 49 times in Matthew's gospel and 16 times in the Gospel of Mark. There are also 38 occurrences in Luke. Something so important to Jesus ought to be understood and ought also to be the primary object of his followers' concern.

A second reason to come to grips with the kingdom of God is that occasionally a critic of contemporary preaching will "wish out loud" that modern-day preachers would "just preach more like Jesus used to preach." Well, if their wish comes true, preaching will indeed undergo a transformation. However, it will not suddenly become the "old-fashioned, hell-fire and brimstone" variety they expect. Instead, it will be preaching almost entirely consumed with the kingdom of God. Therefore, a return to biblical preaching and teaching requires a better understanding of our Lord's favorite subject.

Another reason for our current interest in the kingdom of God is the attention we are giving in these weeks to the Sermon on the Mount. These three chapters form the largest single, unified block of Jesus' teaching in the New Testament. The clear aim of his "sermon" is to describe the monumental impact of God's kingdom upon human life. Anything that has the potential to make the kind of difference in a life that Jesus describes in this sermon deserves our highest regard and most careful notice!

Yet, in spite of its high level of visibility in the New Testament, William Barclay points out that one mystery remains. "The kingdom is described in pictures and analogies and in its demands and effects, but it is never in so many words defined."[1] If we are to ever clear up the confusion surrounding God's kingdom, we must be able to come to some working definitions of it.

I propose that we begin by removing some of the obstacles in the way of our understanding the kingdom of God. In your daily devotional reading, some of you have no doubt noticed that the New Testament uses two phrases: the kingdom of God and the **kingdom of** heaven. The two phrases mean exactly the same thing and you severely complicate matters if you try to make any distinction between them.

The kingdom of heaven is used only by Matthew and for good reason. Matthew was a Jew and devout Jews were hesitant to ever speak the name of God for fear of using it lightly or inappropriately. That would violate the

---

[1] William Barclay, The Plain Man Looks At The Lord's Prayer. (London: Fontana Books, 1964), p 64.

third commandment, prohibiting taking the Lord's name in vain. So instead of referring to the kingdom of God, a Jew would likely use some other word closely associated with God, one which automatically would bring God to mind. The most obvious word is heaven. Mark and Luke were much less influenced by Jewish traditions. For that reason, they did not hesitate to speak forthrightly of the kingdom of God.

Another obstacle to our understanding this significant New Testament teaching is the concept of "kingdom." How much do we actually know about kingdoms? Few of us – if any- have little first hand experience living under a king or queen. Those who have, have never experienced the kind of oppression and arbitrary terrorism that rulers once inflicted upon their subjects.

For instance, Henry VIII of England once stripped a man of his property and title for simply laughing at the wrong time. France's Louis XIV imprisoned a man for life because he didn't like his appearance. Tamerlane, the Mongol ruler, destroyed whole cities that didn't please him and erected enormous pyramids with the inhabitants' skulls. Most ancient people, including those who lived during Jesus' earthly lifetime, lived under such absolute monarchs. [2]

If we are to understand the kingdom of God, we must realize that there are both similarities and dissimilarities between it and earthly kingdoms. Clearly, the kingdom of God cannot be identified with any political power, party, or leader, nor defined by geographical boundaries, nor even established, protected, preserved, threatened, or destroyed by military might. It is the kingdom of God!

You may recall that when Jesus appeared before Pilate on the eve of his crucifixion, he declared that the nature of his kingdom was not like anything else in this world. "My kingdom is not of this world," he said. "If it were, my servants would fight to prevent my arrest by the Jews. But... my kingdom is from another place." (John 18:36) In a moment, I will tell you what he meant.

However, first I must tell you about at least one highly significant similarity between the kingdom of God and the kingdoms of this earth. In a true monarchy, one person's desires and wishes always take precedence over the desires and wishes of every other kingdom subject. Kingdoms are not typically democratic. A consensus is not routinely required. Opinion polls and surveys are

---

[2] John Killinger, The God Named Hallowed. (Nashville: Abingdon Press, 1988), p.34

unnecessary. A majority vote settles absolutely nothing! The only thing that matters in a kingdom is the wish of the king or queen. Like that, the eternal kingdom of God exists solely to do God's will! The eternal kingdom of God is **not democratic**, and God's rule cannot be overturned by majority vote!

Do you recall what Jesus taught his followers to pray in the model prayer? Wasn't it, "Your kingdom come, Your will be done, on earth as it is in heaven?" Do you know what that means? Think about it. Is it even conceivable that anybody in heaven would do anything contrary to the will of God? Certainly, the angels do His will. The saints do His will. The Son does His will. Everybody does God's will in heaven! No exceptions. It is not like our world, where very few people do His will and none of us do it perfectly.

But apparently, that is to be our prayer – and the aim of our life: to do His will on earth as perfectly as it is done in heaven! Imagine that, if you can. If you can, it helps immensely toward arriving at that mysterious, much-needed definition of the kingdom of God. Try this definition. Write it down, preferably in the margin of your Bible next to the text, or beside this particular petition in the model prayer. The kingdom of God is life lived completely under the lordship of Jesus, both now and in the age to come.

If you accept that definition, it means several important things. First, it means that you understand that you can be a part of God's kingdom even while walking down the streets of North Augusta. It also means that you understand your obligation to yield your life – not partially, nor mostly, but entirely – to the sovereignty of God. It means that you understand completely that God is more than your partner, and you must give Him more than token cooperation, or occasional permission to intrude in your affairs. It means that He is the absolute Ruler over your life and you must be entirely submitted to Him!

This definition also underscores the urgency of the message of Jesus and John the Baptist. (Matthew 3:1) The kingdom of God is indeed very near! It's very important that you listen to me at this point. The coming of God's kingdom dawned with Jesus' first coming!

We're like the Jews of Jesus' day. They kept talking about the signs of the kingdom's coming. They kept looking for changes in the heavens, eruptions in the mountains, great and cataclysmic shifts in the power balance of the world's political order. Hearing all of their endless speculation and arguments, Jesus finally countered:

> *"The kingdom of God is not coming with signs to be observed; nor will they say, "Lo,*

here it is!" or "There!" for behold the kingdom of God is in the midst of you." Luke 17:20-21)

Imagine that! It was already there – right under their noses, in fact, and they didn't even know it. - So close to them that they could reach out and touch it, and they weren't even aware of it.

There is an ancient story about how God hid the true meaning of life. It says that before He created the first human being, God discussed with his angels where He could hide life's meaning. He did not want it to be found too easily but only after a great deal of trouble and search.

One of the angels suggested that the secret should rest at the bottom of the sea. Another advocated placing it in the bowels of the earth, and a third recommended that it be hidden on the highest mountain summit. A fourth angel argued that humans were created with enough intelligence that they would eventually search out all of these places. God agreed and said, "The only place that human beings will never dream of looking for the secret of life is in the hardest place to see – within themselves."

Imagine that, the kingdom is already here - in Christ! It's a bit baffling, but it's true. The kingdom of God is not just some future reality, but it can be experienced right now! In fact, it's already here, within those who pray and really mean it, "Thy kingdom come, Thy will be done on earth as it is in heaven." None of us is very far from God's kingdom at this very moment and place. In fact, it's so close that you could reach out and touch it. You could receive it into your heart and soul at this very moment – for it's there that the kingdom finds its true home.

Do you understand what I am telling you? You are much closer than you think to entering the kingdom of God, to becoming the person that God wants you to be – much, much closer! All that stands between you and His kingdom is you willingness to do two things: one, make up your mind that His kingdom is what you really want, and two, demonstrate your willingness to pay the price for admission.

Do you remember the rest of the sermon Jesus preached? It wasn't just the announcement that the kingdom of God has come. He also laid down the singular condition for entering that kingdom. "Repent!" He said. It's time that you and I understand that it's repentance and the kingdom of God which go hand in hand, not respectability, hard work, nor even self-righteousness. The burden of repentance is placed upon each of us – as much upon the shoulders of the religious and spiritual elite, the socially acceptable and culturally approved, as upon the backs of those who are more obviously godless and more openly rebellious.

Repentance is the price of admission to the kingdom of God. It means that we come to our senses and realize that we cannot keep going the same way we are going and ever get to His kingdom. It means that we realize that we are headed in the wrong direction and so, we turn completely around and go in the opposite direction if we are to ever see the kingdom of God. It means that we do an about face, a dramatic reversal if we ever hope to enter His kingdom.

I warn you. If you find it difficult, it's probably because you are satisfied with what you have and who you are, and frankly, you see no need to change. It may be that you have so much and are so comfortable with the way things are that you don't want anything to change. Jesus once said that it's harder for a rich man to get into the kingdom of heaven than for a camel to squeeze through the eye of a needle. He knew, didn't he? When you are on top of the mountain, you don't always need God. Oh, we want the kingdom to come, just not now! We want it to come – but not if it's going to disrupt our lives and interfere with the way we do things. We want the kingdom to come – on earth, in everybody else, just not in us, not yet!

On the Sunday after Hurricane Andrew devastated South Dade County, Florida, a pastor stood to preach to an overflow congregation in the yard next to where their sanctuary used to stand. Their community had been destroyed and so had their church. There was not a person in the neighborhood who had not been deeply touched by the devastation. Most had lost their homes and their businesses – along with all of their personal belongings. The pastor preached in a T-shirt and shorts – all that he had to wear. He preached on the phrase from the Model Prayer – "Thy kingdom come." "How can those words possibly hold any meaning for us today?" he asked. "Our lives are in shambles."

But he continued. "The truth is, we can now understand the need for the kingdom better than we ever could before. Before, our lives were safe, happy, well-ordered. But now we realize how quickly it can all be lost. Now the roof over our head is gone. The telephones don't work. There's no electricity. The doctor's offices have blown away. We have little food and many don't even have their own clothes. Now there is just us and God. And we have found – in the depths, in the darkness and terror – that His kingdom remains and shelters us all!"

Are you in the depths? Are you at the end of your rope? Do you have nowhere else to turn? Has everything been lost? The good news is that the kingdom of God is eternal, and it's big enough to shelter you. It's here now, closer than you ever dreamed. Why don't you come on in?

BRINGING OUT THE BEST IN US
Matthew 5:13-16

WHEN HE WAS SEVEN YEARS OLD, his schoolteacher washed her hands entirely of Thomas Edison. In her view, he was a hopeless case. One day, in the boy's presence, she told an inspector that Thomas was "addled" and that there simply was no point in his attending school anymore.

One of Abraham Lincoln's teachers said about him, "When you consider that Abe has had only four months of school, he is very good with his studies, but he is a daydreamer and asks foolish questions."

One teacher told Woodrow Wilson's parents: "Woodrow is a unique member of the class. He is ten years old and is only beginning to learn to read and write. He shows signs of improving, but you must not set your sights too high for him."

Another teacher gave her assessment of Albert Einstein: "Albert is a very poor student. He is mentally slow, unsociable, and is always daydreaming. He is spoiling it for the rest of the class. Frankly, it would be in the best interests of all if he were removed from school at once."

Amelia Earhart grew up to become a pioneer aviator. However, one of her teachers told her mother, "I am very concerned about Amelia. She is bright and full of curiosity, but her interest in bugs and other crawling things and her daredevil projects are just not fitting for a young lady. Perhaps we could channel her curiosity into a safe hobby."

Caruso's teacher told him that he had no voice. Admiral Byrd was retired from the Navy as "unfit for service." And an editor told Louisa May Alcott that she would "never be able to write anything for popular consumption."[3]

It is amazing how frequently great men and women have been misjudged in their earlier years – not just by teachers, but by parents and peers, by family friends, and even clergy. Fortunately, somewhere in the course of their personal development, someone else saw something else entirely and helped to pull it out of them.

That's what strikes me most about this portion of the Sermon on the Mount. This little insignificant handful of people was suddenly cast upon the world's stage and told that they were going to make an unprecedented and

---

[3] Alan Loy McGinnis, The Power of Optimism. (San Francisco: Harper and Row Publishers, 1990), pp. 38-39.

incomparable impact upon human history! They were told that they were a force with which the world would have to reckon. It's absolutely remarkable to me that Jesus would say those kinds of things to such an unassuming group of followers. And yet, because he did I have a great deal more hope for the future!

The text tells me that people who find themselves and their personal worth in relationship with Jesus – and not primarily within themselves – are given the gift of feeling themselves of worldwide worth. That's just one of the things that conversion to the Christian faith does for a person! It clarifies the reason a person is here. It defines the purpose – the mission – of his or her life.

Have you ever wondered why you were born? Have you discovered your purpose in life yet? Everyone has one, although very few know what theirs is. What's yours? Why are you here? Let me help you move in the direction of finding your purpose in life and discovering why God gave you this wonderful gift in the first place.

Before I begin, let me tell you what a statement of your life's purpose ought to look like. You should be able to sum up your life's purpose in just a few words. It usually begins with "I am..." and states in a simple way why you're here and what you are here to do.

Now, listen. It is important that you understand that your purpose is not the same as all the goals of your life. Goals – like graduating from high school and college, being happily married and raising children, making a million dollars in a wonderful job, having a beautiful home, spoiled grandchildren, wonderful friends, a place at the beach, perhaps even another place in the mountains, and a reasonably comfortable retirement – are all worthy and noble ambitions. However, if that is all you live for, you will never be satisfied and happy even if you succeed at achieving all your goals.

Do you remember the young, successful and very rich man who came to Jesus one day asking about eternal life? (Mark 10:17-31) Perhaps he was the first yuppie. Just like most contemporary yuppies, he was aware that something truly significant was missing from his life. His affluence and success had left him empty. His quest for religious and moral excellence had not even fulfilled him. He was a miserable human being and he was willing to do almost anything to escape the misery.

But there was one thing he was unwilling to do which kept him from realizing the reason he was born. His riches kept him from God. He was so wrapped up in his possessions that he couldn't bear to separate himself from them. What he owned, he discovered owned him. He did not know where his things ended and he began.

Most of us are just like that. We are so wrapped up in that we do, where we work and live, and what we have that those aspects of life have become our primary identity. Introduce yourself to ten strangers and ask them to tell you about themselves. I suspect that all ten will begin by telling you where they work, where they live, as well as the number, names and ages of their family members. However, after they tell you their name, almost nothing else they say will begin with the simple, self-revealing words, "I am...." Our lives are so intertwined with what we do and what we have, where we live and how we earn our keep, that we really don't know who we are apart from those categories. That's part of what makes it so difficult when the kids leave home and we reach retirement. Who are we really apart from our family and our work?

Somewhere along the way we get the notion that our primary purpose in life is to keep busy doing something, working toward some goal, and accomplishing some task. However, according to the Bible, our real mission in life is to **be** something. In the words of the text, we were sent here to **be** the salt of the earth and the light of the world. **That** is our primary mission.

And it's all wrapped up in our relationship with God, not in what we do and what we own. You can read all the self-help and positive thinking books you want. You can attend all the motivational seminars you like and still come away with only short-term happiness and fleeting satisfaction. You can hop from one relationship to another. You can change jobs every six months and in spite of it all, still experience a pervasive emptiness and restlessness in the core of your being.

No wonder your frustration mounts. Nothing seems to bring you lasting happiness. Several years ago, one of the Super Bowl champion Washington Redskins expressed that frustration. It was at the end of the season after the team had won their last championship. The new season had not been kind to them. The Redskins didn't even make it through the play-offs. One of their players said, "If winning the Super Bowl is what life is all about, then why does it have to be won all over again every year?"

You know what he meant, don't you? Isn't there something that lasts? Isn't there anything that ties it all together and helps make sense of it all? Isn't there something that stays won?

Yes, and that's what this passage is all about! It's about who you are and why you're here. It's about your mission, the reason you were born. Don't you see? Mission is not just one part of Christian discipleship- an optional part that you can take or leave. Mission – purpose – is essentially what Christian discipleship is all about. Christians are people who have discovered in their relationship with God through Jesus Christ, precisely why they were born and what they are doing here.

Look at it again. Jesus does not tell his disciples that they should be, ought to be, or must become the salt of the earth and the light of the world. Simply by virtue of the fact that they have come in contact with him, they are different! Christians who are Christians are the salt of the earth! It is a straightforward statement of fact. Jesus tells his disciples who they are before he ever tells them what he expects of them. It's the way he brings out the best in them – and us!

For 12 years, the Green Bay Packers had won only 30% of their games. By 1958, their record had dropped to a dismal one and ten. Then, in 1959, a new coach came along -Vince Lombardi. During Lombardi's nine-year tenure, the Packers had nine winning seasons, beat their opponents 75% of the time, and walked away with five NFL championships, including the first two Super Bowls.

What made the difference? It wasn't what Coach Lombardi knew. Several other coaches in the league knew just as much about strategy and tactics as did he. He had an extraordinary ability to motivate his players. Frank Gifford says that Lombardi could get an extra ten percent out of every player. "Multiply ten percent times forty men on the team times fourteen games in a season – and you're going to win."[4]

It's like someone else said: Treat a man as he appears to be and you make him worse. But treat a man as if he already were what he potentially could be, and you make him everything he should be." Isn't that what Jesus did with his first disciples? Isn't that exactly what he tries to do with you and me?

It makes no difference what others say or think about you. It makes no difference what you think or feel about yourself. Your circumstances – no matter how impossible they seem to you – don't even present an obstacle to finding the reason you are here. If you are a Christian, you are the salt of the earth and the light of the world! That's the truth.

Now, here's the challenge. Salt is either salty, or it's not. If it's not salty, it's not worthy of the name. It's simply thrown out the door. The application is obvious, isn't it? While Christians are not challenged to become salty – our saltiness is a gift of God's grace – we are challenged to **stay** salt, to act like salt, to **be** real Christians.

It's a warning intended to shake Christians out of out complacency. As salt and light, our mission is to be different, but also to **make a difference** in the world.

---

[4] Alan Loy McGinnis, <u>Bringing Out The Best In People</u>.
(Minneapolis: Augsburg Publishing House, 1985). pp. 25-26.

There are pressures at work and school – all around us and within us, in fact – not to be too Christian and not to take our faith too seriously. Although we are salt because of our new nature, there is constant pressure to be insipid salt, to use some common sense when it comes to our faith, and to be "normal" people. Some of that is the work of the Holy Spirit Who never intends for us to be obnoxious, mean, or intolerable in expressing our faith. But some of it can also be the work of the spirit that makes people cowards, especially fearful of what others will say and think of them.

Several years ago, there was a Peanuts cartoon strip featuring a dialogue between Lucy and Charlie Brown. In the first frame, Lucy asks Charlie Brown if he has ever known anyone who was really happy. Before she could even finish her sentence, Snoopy comes dancing into the frame. He dances, and spins and bounces his way across two frames of the cartoon strip. Finally, in the last frame, Lucy finishes her sentence with the words, "...and was still in his right mind?"

Christians are people who have been changed by the power of God at work in Jesus Christ. They are people who have discovered who they are, why they are here, and what they are supposed to be doing. Because of that, they're also people who are really happy – and in their right mind!

It certainly makes a difference in your own daily struggles. Once you know your purpose – to be salt and light, to bring glory to God through your good work – it becomes a sort of divining rod. When you're wondering, "Should I do this or do that?" it helps to be able to look at your purpose. If one choice is in line with your purpose and the other is not, the decision has already been made. And if neither is in line with your purpose, look for other options.

Listen to the words of the Lord: "You are the salt of the earth... You are the light of the world....that men may see your good works and glorify Your Father in heaven." That is who you are and why you're here. Only two questions remain. One, does it make a difference in the way you put your life together? And two, does the way you live make a difference in the world?

Is your life characterized by "that certain something"? No one can really put their finger on it, but it's the reason you stand out from the crowd. It's the reason you make a positive difference in your home, in your place of business, at school, and in the community. Wellington reportedly said that when Napoleon was on the battlefield, his presence was in balance, the equivalent of fighting against another 40.000 soldiers. Does the power of the presence of God in you carry that much weight?

It makes that kind of difference when you know why you're here. You know now, don't you?

WHAT RELIGION ARE YOU?

Matthew 5:17-20

TWO OF THE MOST FAMOUS CHRISTIAN preachers were contemporaries during the nineteenth century. D.L. Moody was a great American evangelist and pastor. Charles H. Spurgeon literally took Great Britain by storm through his powerful preaching of the gospel.

D.L. Moody went to London to meet Spurgeon, whom he had admired from a distance and considered to be his professional mentor. However, when Spurgeon answered the door with a cigar in his mouth, Moody fell down the stairs in shock. "How could you, a man of God, smoke that?" protested the great American evangelist.

Spurgeon took the stogie out of his mouth and walked to the steps where Moody was still standing in bewilderment. Putting his fingers on Moody's rather rotund stomach, he smiled and said: "The same way that you, a man of God, could be that fat!"[5]

---

[5] Stephen Brown, When Being Good Isn't Good Enough. (Nashville: Thomas Nelson Publishers, 1990), p.87.

Obviously, the word Christian means different things to different people. It always has. In the late New Testament era, some believed that all Christians should worship on the seventh day of the week. Some others thought it more appropriate to worship on the first day since that coincided with the resurrection of Jesus. Some thought it was completely inappropriate for Christians to knowingly buy meat which had been dedicated by pagan priests to the worship of pagan idols. Others felt just as conscientiously that since the idols were harmless and the gods they represented were non-existent, the meat was not tainted in the least. In fact, it would be a shame to let such high quality meat go to waste or be consumed by others. (Romans 14:1-8)

Even before those differences of opinion developed, Jesus was criticized for his apparent indifference toward prevailing notions of spirituality. Many were suspicious of his orthodoxy. He simply wasn't conservative enough for them. In reality, he just didn't agree with most of their pet theories. He didn't honor the sabbath day the way they did. (Mark 2:23-3:6) He ignored their rules about fasting. (Mark 2:18) He openly defied the time-honored rituals related to how you wash your hands and dishes on a religious holiday. (Mark 7:1-5) And to their way of thinking, the worst thing he did was to associate with low-class people. He actually ate with them and gave the impression that he enjoyed being around them. (Luke 15:1)

To people who placed their rules of etiquette above the Ten Commandments, Jesus was impolite, uncouth, impious, and irreligious. Worse than that, in the eyes of the highly regarded, conservative religious elite of his day, he was clearly a law-breaker, a very dangerous criminal.

When he preached this sermon, Jesus tried to set the record straight. He told his critics: "Don't be so quick to jump to the wrong conclusion. I have not come to destroy the law and the prophets (which, by the way, was practically their entire Bible). I have come to fulfill it." (v. 17, my paraphrase)

Jesus has no quarrel with the law of God. He had come to do it – to "fill it full" of meaning through his own obedience. He had come to establish it more permanently, not to set it aside. "As long as heaven and earth last," he said, "the Law will not become passé'." (v.18, my paraphrase) Likewise, serious followers of Jesus cannot be anti-law or indifferent to scripture. Jesus lived out of it and for it. So must we. The Law gave him directions for his life and it remains our most reliable guide.

His quarrel was with what had happened to the Law in the people's hands. The scribes and Pharisees were meticulous definers. They could tell to the smallest degree exactly what the commandments of God meant. They had worked diligently to dot "i" and cross every "t". For instance, when the law said, "Remember the sabbath day, to keep it holy," they could tell precisely what you could do on the Sabbath and still keep the Law.

In the process, several unfortunate things happened. First, these interpretations eventually were given equal standing with the original commandments of God. In fact, that's how the Law came to be so expansive. In Jesus' day, the Law contained 613 commandments. Their understanding and interpretations of it were included alongside it. It was inevitable, then, that the Law was put in God's place. In fact, the Law became their God and their God became the Law.

Jesus called for a different kind of righteousness which exceeded the righteousness of the scribes and Pharisees – not in terms of religious excesses, but in the most unusual and extraordinary was of all. He called for the fulfillment of the Law through personal communion with God. You may recall that on a later occasion, Jesus said that everything in the Law was aimed at just two objectives: to get people to love the Lord their God with all their heart and soul, with all their mind and strength, and to love their neighbors as themselves. (Matthew 22:37-40)

In the kind of environment in which we live, Christians need especially to hear and heed this teaching of Jesus, along with its inherent warnings. Ours is a confusing day of resurgent conservatism. A large part of the problem is that we have noticed that conservative politics and religious belief no longer necessarily indicate conservative lifestyle and morality. That makes this section of the Sermon on the Mount all the more relevant. There are very real dangers in Pharisaical fundamentalism and radical legalism. To help us find our way through these confusing times, I want to remind you of several basic, biblical truths. Be sure to listen carefully to each.

First, it is essential that you understand that legalism is not the way to get to God. It will not save you. The Apostle Paul countered this heresy among the Ephesians. To them, he wrote: "...it is by grace that you have been saved, through faith- it is not from yourselves...- not by your works, so that none of you can boast." (2:8-9)

Listen! Salvation that requires human achievement, hard work, personal effort – no matter how noble and honorable – salvation based upon religious exercises, is heresy! What's essentially wrong with it is that it is a system in which a person gets the glory for the achievement, not God! It's more concerned with externals than internals, with being seen by others when Jesus said a person ought to be happy even if no one really knows what's going on except God. The reason radical conservatism persists today is because it appeals so strongly to our pride.

If you think about it, you'll realize that practically every cult focuses upon earning salvation by doing certain things. If you will stand on a street corner long enough, give out so many tracts or pamphlets, if you will sacrifice so much of your time, if you will be baptized, or contribute your money, if you will pray or attend a certain number of meetings, then one day your good works and hard work will pay off. God will smile on you. And who knows? Ultimately, when the good stuff in your life is weighed against the bad, all the things you do may tip the scales in your favor and you'll get in, even if it is by the skin of your teeth.

Let me be absolutely straight with you. You are saved by grace. The reason it takes grace is because you have nothing to give, nothing to earn, nothing to pay that is worthy of salvation. It is a free gift. So stop tolerating the heretical gospel of works. It's legalism, it's wrong, and it will kill you!

The second biblical truth is this: legalism does not sanctify you. In other words, your personal goodness, conservatism, or orthodoxy does not bring you to God and it will not keep you there, either. Legalism is no guarantee that you are now close to God, nor that you will stay close to God. Most of us know that in our minds but have a great deal of trouble believing it with our hearts.

The Apostle Paul told Timothy to avoid people who have "a form of godliness," but have no spiritual substance or reality to back it up. (2 Timothy 3:5) Genuine godliness flows naturally out of a vital relationship with God through Jesus Christ. However, simply trying to act godly will never create that relationship.

This ought to be of real concern to parents and grandparents. If you really want to mess up the minds of your children, then raise them in an atmosphere where spiritual performance and pretension are more important than reality. In other words, fake your faith. Sneak around and pretend that you are spiritual. By your example, train your children to do the same. Embrace a list of dos and don'ts publicly but hypocritically practice them privately – and never own up to the fact that it's hypocrisy. Say one thing and live another, and you can count on it! Emotional and spiritual damage will occur. What's more, when they're free to make their own choices, your children will likely become cynical, skeptical, and very bitter toward God and His church.

Charles Swindoll tells of a missionary family who resigned their post, returned to the United States, and gave up God's call over a jar of peanut butter. The place where they were sent to serve did not have peanut butter, but they happened to enjoy peanut butter a great deal. They made arrangements with some of their friends in the States to send them peanut butter every now and then so they could enjoy it between meals.

The problem is that they didn't know until they started receiving the supply of peanut butter that the other missionaries considered it a mark of spirituality to go without peanut butter. The new missionary family didn't agree. They kept getting their peanut butter, but they didn't advertise it. They enjoyed it in the privacy of their own home. But the pressure intensified. The other missionaries became so petty and unbelievably small-minded, they treated the new family with so much meanness that it finally just finished off the young missionary family.[6]

That's a classic example of narrow, squint-eyed legalism. Legalism is a killer. It kills a congregation when the pastor is legalistic. People with their rigid lists of dos and don'ts kill the spirit of joy and spontaneity in those who want to enjoy their new life in Jesus Christ.

Would you please give up your list of dos and don'ts for everybody else? Keep it to yourself. If you're not into peanut butter – or square dancing, shag dancing, going to movies, or other things Christians enjoy – that's

---

[6] Charles R. Swindoll, The Grace Awakening. (Dallas: Word Publishing, 1990), p. 93.

fine. It's great. If that's your thing, you shouldn't do it. But don't tell someone else they can't enjoy it. And don't judge them because they do. Whether they do or don't, it's no indication of their spirituality.

Third., legalism – conservatism – is not a true reflection of the heart. Jesus told the scribes and Pharisees: "You are truly like whitewashed tombs which indeed appear beautiful outwardly, but inside you are full of dead men's bones and all uncleanness." (Matthew 23:27)

Have you ever met anyone who does everything right? They never step out of line? When they talk about sin, it's almost as if they're speaking as an outsider of the human race. Well, let me tell you something. I've been a pastor for twenty-three years. I've met some of these people along the way, and many of them are as mean as snakes. Their hearts are so distorted you wouldn't believe it. They do it right on the outside, but inside they are filled with bitterness, criticism, and hatred. They have no hesitation in spreading gossip, twisting the truth, or damaging reputations. Doing everything right on the outside is certainly not an accurate measurement of a person's heart.

Fourth, the Law of God is not intended to be used as a weapon against other members of the family of God. Paul warned the Romans: "...You are inexcusable..whoever you are the judge, for in whatever you judge another, you condemn yourself; for you who judge practice the same things." (Romans 2:1)

You already know this, but I need you to know that I know it too. If you look for the bad things in me, you'll find them. You won't even have to make them up. I'm a lot better than I used to be, but I've got so far to go that you won't have to work very hard to find something to criticize.

But before you start loading your gun, let me tell you something else. You aren't all that hot yourself. In all honesty, what we have here is a "Mexican Stand Off." We both have loaded guns and we both make very good targets. We both must rely upon the grace of God to save us, right?

Petty Christians have lost their focus. They've turned their eyes away from what matters most and search furiously to find things that don't matter at all. The result is that the rest of us live in fear of them – in fear of their judgment, their criticism, their attacks. It's time we remember that we all stand under the judgment of God. And frankly, if it were not for His grace, we would all be in the same doomed boat.

Sadly, many people who think they are Christians have never really faced the question of how they stand before God. They've assumed, like the scribes and the

Pharisees, that if a person does this, that, and the other, they're all right. They've assumed that if a person always comes out on the conservative side of any moral or spiritual issue, or if they consistently agree with the conservative viewpoint in political or cultural debates, they're all right. They've never really thought about God. They've never really considered that they need a personal relationship with Him.

Yet that relationship is what the Kingdom of God is all about. And the moment you realize it, there's not much point in telling me what you eat or don't eat. There's not much point in telling me that you drink or don't drink, whether you dance or you don't. It just doesn't matter how much better you think you are than prostitutes and drunkards.

The Christian faith is not about your little bit of goodness, or mine; not what I do or do not do; not how much better I am than somebody else; nor even how much better I am than I used to be. To get into the kingdom of God, you forget all about who you are and what you've done. You realize that it's not your morality, nor even your ideas of what's right and what's wrong – not even how you think others should live –that saves you. To get into His Kingdom, it takes His grace – nothing more!

ARE YOU PRONE TO BLOWING YOUR FUSE?
Matthew 5:21-26

I HAD JUST FINISHED SPEAKING to a local professional organization when one of the members asked if she could talk with me for a few minutes. Both her tone and facial expression told me that whatever was on her mind was significantly urgent. We found a quiet corner of the large meeting room. By the time we got there, she was crying quietly.

"I have to talk to somebody," she said. She went on to describe an argument she had with her husband earlier that day. It all started over nothing really important. In fact, she admitted that it could have been avoided altogether. Certainly, it could have been handled differently, but it hadn't been. Angry, hostile, and ugly words had been spoken.

"I got so mad that I couldn't see straight," she said. "I was out of control. When I left, he was sweeping up broken glass from the kitchen floor. I actually threw a glass at him. I'm so ashamed of myself."

Her crying became more intense. Her angry outburst had left her absolutely devastated. She really didn't know what to do. Finally, she composed herself enough to say, "You know, I'm a Christian. But sometimes I feel as if God converted every part of me except my temper. I try to do what's right, but I admit that I have a terrible temper. It seems to be getting worse. It's sure not getting any better. I get so angry!"

What do you think? What would you have told her? Is it sinful to be angry – always? Clearly, anger can be sinful. It can become a spiritual cancer. It can destroy us and devastate other people. It can disrupt families, ruin friendships, split churches, and start wars. Anger is a powerful force which, more often that not, is released in negative and destructive ways.

In this section of the Sermon on the Mount, Jesus addresses the problem of human anger. You must remember that in the verses immediately preceding these, he tells his audience that authentic spirituality is a matter of the heart, not outward appearance. Scribes and Pharisees are concerned about how things look to other people. Their primary concern is that they always leave a favorable impression. Jesus, however, is concerned about how things really are, deep within a person.

So, in the remaining verses of Matthew 5 (vs. 21-48), he demonstrates the practical impact of God upon six everyday situations. The first example Jesus gives describes the difference kingdom living makes in the way we handle our anger. It's a very pragmatic portion of scripture, one whose meaning it is hardly possible to escape.

For instance, decent people never think of murdering another person. People like us just don't think like that. We are horrified, in fact, when someone we know is brutally and senselessly killed. Scribes and Pharisees would never think of murdering anyone either. They were certainly above that. Yet, Jesus indicates that it's not good enough that we have never killed anyone. The kingdom standard requires that we never even wish any harm, misfortune, or bad luck to come to someone else. Such thoughts lead murderers to actually kill.

The Christian life demands that we never even allow a hard feeling toward another person to dwell in our heart. A Christian should never become angry enough to attack another person's character or reputation. In Jesus' view, anger which inflicts hurt is always potentially deadly. That basically means that there's not much difference between a decent man or woman with an out-of-control temper and the callous, cold-blooded murderer. The same destructive emotion lurks in both hearts. And after all, that's what God is most concerned about – the human heart.

In modern translations, Jesus' teaching about anger is organized into three paragraphs. In the first, he describes the kind of anger that concerns God, the anger He condemns. (vs. 21-22) It's a significant part of this teaching because it's very important that you understand that not all anger is wrong, sinful, or even inappropriate. After all, God created us with the capacity anger. There are circumstances in which anger is a natural physiological and emotional response to a perceived danger. In those cases, it's unlikely that you can keep yourself from becoming angry, even if you wanted to.

The Bible also recognizes that there are occasions when anger is entirely appropriate. For instance, the Apostle Paul reminds us in Ephesians that it's possible to "be angry, but sin not." (Ephesians 4:26) Obviously, he is referring to a controlled anger.

He also commended the Corinthians for their outrage against a Christian who had married his stepmother. (1 Corinthians 5;1; 2 Corinthians 7:11) That was righteous indignation against sin; and it was entirely appropriate.

Jesus is perhaps the best example of righteous indignation. When you study how he used and expressed anger, two things are apparent. On the one hand, Jesus was never upset by unkindness directed toward himself. There is no occasion when he ever felt slighted or became personally offended! He was often criticized, questioned, rejected, accused falsely, lied about, pushed around and shoved, taunted, beaten, cursed at, even spat upon, and finally nailed to a cross. According to the Apostle Peter, however, "he never sinned, never told a lie, never answered back when insulted; when he suffered he did not threaten to get even; he left his case in the hands of God...." (1 Peter 2:22-23, TLB)

That does not mean that we are called upon to let other people abuse us. In fact, if you are currently in an abusive situation – if you are suffering physical, emotional, and verbal abuse – you ought to report it and get out of it as soon as you can. What I am pointing out is that Jesus' anger was never selfish and neither should ours be.

On the other hand, Jesus did become outraged when he witnessed injustices toward others. When he saw other people being exploited, or mistreated, cheated or hurt, he became upset! When he saw a sinful woman being judged without mercy, he became angry. That, however, is the primary difference between his style of anger and ours. We are quick to take personal offense and become outraged over it. However, seldom do we notice when others are exploited or mistreated.

The Bible condemns two kinds of anger. One is represented by the word, "thumos", and describes the kind of anger which flares up suddenly and the dies out just as quickly. You frequently see it in the checkout line at a supermarket, on the golf course, the basketball court, the softball field, or in the middle of traffic. It's what folks around Griffin, Georgia – where I grew up –referred to as a "fit", or a "tantrum."

All ages and both genders are susceptible to "thumos." The man who flies into a rage because his toast is burnt or his coffee is lukewarm is having a"fit." So is the teenager who runs to her room, slams the door behind her, and throws herself on the bed in crocodile tears because she can't go to the ball game, but had to stay home and study for a test. The church member who quits the church because his announcement was left out of the bulletin, or her name was left off some list, is pitching the proverbial "fit."

People who are short-tempered, hostile, and irritable are basically immature. They may be adult sized in their physical development and adult-aged chronologically. But people who throw fits are emotionally little children and still scream, kick, and create scenes when they don't get their way.

It's not cute. In fact, it's pathetic. And worse, the Apostle Paul describes a temper tantrum as the work of the devil. In fact, he catalogues it right alongside fornication, idolatry, sorcery, and drunkenness. (Galatians 5:19-21; Ephesians 4:31) If you're prone to sudden outbursts of temper, you need to grow up. It's put you in some pretty bad company. Besides that, it's killing you!

The other kind of anger described in the Bible is "orge". It's the word used in the text, in fact. It's a brooding kind of anger – the kind a person feeds, cultivates, and will not allow to die. It's the kind of anger which refuses to forgive – which says, "No matter how long it takes me, I'll get even. I'll get 'em back eventually, one way or the other." It stews and simmers and boils over a long period of time. It never forgets!

In verse 22, Jesus describes how "orge" usually works. Typically, it works on undermining another person's self-worth and self-image through expressions of contempt. The word "raca" is really more a sound than it is a word. It was the sound a person makes when they clear their throat in order to spit. In the first century, it was considered the meanest thing one person could do to another. If you cleared your throat as if to spit in the direction of another, it was the same thing as if you said, "You had better get out of my sight before I spit in your face."

The Greek word for "fool" is related to our word "moron." It, too, was an expression of meanness and contempt, and was clearly used with the intention to hurt someone else.

We have lots of ways that we express that kind of anger today. Tragically, the place where most of our deepest anger is expressed is in the home. Family members really do inflict a lot of hurt on one another, even when we don't mean to. It's not that we're really all that mad at each other. We don't intend to make the people we love so much the targets of our anger. It's just that they always happen to be there – in the way – when we're most angry. One of the most common experiences of life is to innocently and unknowingly walk into the fall-out of another person's frustration. Suddenly, all their anger comes pouring out.

Listen! If the family is going to survive, the name-calling, the bickering, the constant put-downs, the meanness, the erosive criticism must stop. Husbands and wives, parents and children, brothers and sisters must put a stop to the degrading things we say to one another. No family member should ever call another family member stupid, gay, a retard, meathead, or anything worse!

For the Christian, the same goes for the workplace and the church. We often think we are far removed from the murderer's hideous crime. But have you never held another person in contempt? Have you ever wished another person misfortune or bad luck? Have you ever wished some co-worker or employer would lose their job and be forced to move to another city so that you would not have to deal with them anymore? Have you ever wished in the deepest recesses of your heart that someone else were dead, and out of the way? Have you never said, "How could anyone be so stupid?" Jesus said that murder begins with those feelings. And in his view, there's little difference between the hateful, spiteful person and the murderer!

In the second paragraph, Jesus tells us what to do with our anger, and how important it is that we do it. (vs. 23-24) There are several things that can be done. An angry person can always repress their anger – and many do. They deny that they are angry at all. "Angry? Who, me? Don't be silly. I'd never let a little thing like that upset me. Don't give it another thought." All the while, they're keeping a lid on it and it's boiling underneath. Repressed anger – anger held in – often turns in and eventually creates some serious health problems.

An angry person can also suppress their anger. Many do that as well. "Oh, sure. I'll admit that I'm angry. But what can I do about it? If I tell him how I really feel, I'll get fired, sure enough. I'll just keep it to myself until the right opportunity comes along." A person who suppresses their anger admits that they have it, but that it's also not very prudent to express it. They will just go on smiling and pretending. The right moment will come along one day. The problem with that strategy is that suppressed anger tends to come out anyhow. Unfortunately, it is usually directed toward people who are most innocent and least deserving – children, parents, husband or wife, even our best friends.

An angry person can also express their anger. Sometimes they let it all hang out. They don't care who catches it. Their attitude is that the best thing to do is to get it out of your system, to let the chips fall where they may. Somebody else will come along to clean up the aftermath, all the pieces and the mess. After you get it off your mind, it's not your problem anymore. It's someone else's to worry with.

Jesus, however, proposed the best solution. He said that if you're angry, you ought to confess it. Admit it to yourself, admit it to God, and then go to the person toward whom you feel the anger – your husband, your wife, your parents, your friend, your employer – own up to it, and work it out. According to Jesus, that's more important that even finishing what you started here in this place of worship.

What could possible make it that urgent? Jesus explains that in the third paragraph. (vs. 25-26) He draws upon the justice system to make his point. He reasons that if someone brought legal action against you, more than likely, you would try to resolve the issue without ever taking it to court. Most attorneys prefer to reach an "out of court" settlement, if it is at all possible. Once it reaches the court it's essentially out of their hands an in the hands of the judge and jury.

The clear implication of this passage is that unless you deal with your anger now – and resolve it – it will be dealt with before the judgment seat of God. In fact, if your anger toward another person has caused you to sin – even in your heart – that fact alone has guaranteed you time on God's docket. Jesus' clear word of advice is, "If I were you, I'd settle out-of-court!"

IS THERE ANY HARM IN JUST LOOKING?
Matthew 5:27-30

A CLASS OF FOURTH GRADERS was given an overnight assignment to write a paper about their family roots. One little boy asked his mother for help, but he failed to explain that he was working on a homework assignment. She was in the middle of cooking supper when he asked: "Mom, where did I come from?" She thought that he was suddenly curious about where babies come from. But, at that precise moment, that was something she was not prepared to discuss. So, she responded: "Why from the stork honey." The little boy persisted: "Well, where did you come from, Mom?" She responded again, rather uncomfortably: "The stork brought me, too." Once more the little boy asked: "Mom, then where did grandma come from?" The mother's response was the same as before. Finally, the boy went to his room where he began his paper with this sentence: "There hasn't been a natural childbirth in this family for at least three generations."

It's not ever easy to talk about human sexuality, is it? Especially in front of children and strangers, and in public places—like the sanctuary of a church on Sunday mornings. But, I believe that it's imperative that Christians address the serious issues related to human sexuality.

Let me illustrate why I believe that so strongly. I want to ask you a simple question. How many times in a given day do you supposed that you have sexual thoughts? Be sure to consider all the jokes you tell hear, and laugh at, the songs you listen to, sin, and um during the day—country music and contemporary rock—the shows you watch on television—including the movies you rent—the headlines which grab you attention in the local newspaper or in the supermarket check-out lane, and the conversations you have with neighbors and co-workers, or overhear at the hair stylist's. You probably think talk, and are exposed to more sexual influences than you imagined, right? Anything that occupies so much of our thoughts dominates so completely the music and entertainment industries of our land, and is at the root of so much marital, relational, and personal conflict ought to be addressed form a uniquely Christian and biblical perspective.

The focus of this sermon is on of the most misunderstood and trivialized lessons of the New Testament. Does the text really say what is appears to say? And does it really mean what it says? Does it mean that the physical attraction between an unmarried man and woman is sinful even it they do not commit the sinful act/ Does it mean that every sexual thought is dirty and shameful?   Does it men that every admiring look is adulterous?   It so, any one of us escape the scope and breadth of our Lord's judgment?

Let's look at what the text actually says and then determine its meaning and application for our life situation. First it is clear that our Lord clearly intended to redefine the sin of adultery.   That which constituted adultery in His time was radically different from that which constitutes adultery in our own time. In fat, you might be surprised to learn that His world was much more permissive and liberal in its understanding of adultery than ours. And that is precisely the reason a redefinition was needed.

You don't have to read very much of the Old Testament before you discover how rude and uncouth was the understanding of human sexuality in that part of the world. The patriarchs, Abraham, Isaac, and Jacob each had concubines (Genesis 16:1; 30:7), the equivalent of a modern-day mistress, or a live-in surrogate mother. If a man's wife was unable to bear children or if she had not given birth to any son, he was permitted to own a concubine. Her sole purpose was to produce male descendants.

Besides that, many prominent figures and folk heroes had several wives and some openly used the services or prostitutes, and nobody much cared. No fingers were pointed at Samson for his sexual escapades in the boudoirs of the Philistines (Judges 6). No one mentioned that Judah was a married man when he slept with his widowed daughter-in-law while under the mistaken impression that she was a prostitute (Genesis 38:12ff). So long as a man did not sleep with another man's wife, he had not committed adultery, no mater how widespread his philandering.

In that part of the world, adultery was a sin committed against a married man, not even, and never against a woman, including a man's own wife. The law declared that a woman was a man's property. She was the property of her father until such time as she was married. Upon her marriage ownership was transferred to her husband in exchange for other property or services of equal value. Even the tenth commandment prohibiting the coveting by one man of another man's property listed his wife in the inventory of protected personal property, alongside his livestock and servants (Exodus 20:17). Essentially, adultery was a violation of the property law. Its primary concern was with a husband's rights to have children who were unquestionably his own. His wife's adultery with another man seriously compromised his right to that confidence. It was considered such a serious violation of the law that both the adulteress and the adulterer were put to death (Leviticus 20:10: Deuteronomy 22:22).

By the time of Jesus' ministry, the practices of concubinage and multiple marriages had been discontinued. But the double standard still existed . The woman was still regarded as a man's property. She had no rights, no standing of her own! Adultery was still considered an offense against a married man but not a woman, including a man's own wife.

In the text, our Lord clearly objects to the uncivilized and in human treatment of women, not just married women, but women in general who were treated by men as property to be owned, traded, or discarded! To treat any person as merely a sex object is sinful, even when that woman is you wife or that man is your husband! In other words on the basis of his redefinition, it is possible for a man to be guilty of adultery even with his own wife. It's even possible to be guilty of adultery when no physical, sexual act has been committed. In the eyes of our Lord adultery is essentially any attitude which demeans, disgraces, debases or humiliates the worth and integrity of another human being!

It's clear then, that Jesus is primarily concerned to elevate the relationship between men and women to a new level of sacredness and to establish a new and higher degree of mutual respect between them. In the process, he sounds an ominous warning to those who use sex to control, dominate, and manipulate another human being. His warning is to husbands and wives who have little or no contact and virtually no meaningful relationship, with each other outside the bedroom. He calls them to recapture the holy element of intimacy and love which is at the heart o every Christian marriage, a degree of intimacy which can even raise their physical relationship to new levels of spirituality. His warning is to unmarried men and women who share a physical relationship intended only for marriage. He calls them to a serious re-evaluation of their commitment to thief Lord and to each other. He reminds them to establish enduring relationships between Christian men and women. He warns teenagers and young adults for whom sex is merely a way of relieving boredom or acting out their deeper needs. He reminds them that when sex is used to play "control games" with others, when it is merely a means of holding on to a boyfriends or a girlfriend it becomes a destructive force of exploitation and that is the root evil of lust and adultery!

No, Jesus does not prohibit a casual, polite, and admiring glance at a beautiful woman or a handsome man.

Lust is far more serious than that! Generally speaking, it refers to any all-consuming desire. Whenever any urge becomes so over powering that it dominates a person's mind then lust has taken hold. If you have trouble concentrating on anything else other than the one thing you want most right now-- whether it's fame or fortune, a new car or boat, a new house or business a promotion or recognition, a romantic relationship or merely a friendship with another person—it you would do **almost anything** to have what you want—if you would be tempted to risk everything you now have in order to gain what you don't have—you are at the mercy of lust.

In the text, Jesus focused specifically upon the danger of lust when it becomes attached to our human sexuality. When that happens, lust distorts and perverts everything else. A lustful person lives in a perpetual sexual stew. Sexual thoughts and urges dominate the mind, determine behavior, and infiltrate practically every conversation. Lust is not normal sexual desire. It is instead, the all-consuming, selfish and insatiable desire which sees, and if given the opportunity, uses other people as sexual objects.

It's easy to recognize lust. It characterizes the men and women with whom you work or go to school, the ones who seem to have nothing else but sexual thoughts. Everything they say, every joke they tell has an erotic twist. Lust distinguishes men who fall all over themselves and embarrass their wife by their behavior in shopping malls restaurants, and other public places as they gawk at every young, attractive, fashionable dressed female they see. Lust can also describe the friendship between married men and married women. Both are committed to someone else and neither would ever be unfaithful to their spouse. Yet the basic content of their secretive conversations with each other, the essential substance of their friendship enters around flirting, teasing, and sharing the most intimate fantasies and desires, the most personal frustrations and problems with their spouse. Lust motivates the "sneak peek" at *Playboy* or *Playgirl* at the airport newsstand or the bookstore in the local mall. Lust motivates much of the business at local video stores. And it's lust that is at the root of thoughts you would never express, thoughts you can't even believe you think.

Lust is serious business. It's demeaning, degrading debasing, humiliating and shameful. It really shouldn't be trivialized, sneered at, smirked over, and smiled about. The Bible doesn't dismiss it nearly so casually as the wife who tells her husband that there's no harm in looking so long as you don't touch. The Bible doesn't excuse it with a flippancy based upon the argument that everybody lusts, everybody occasionally looks, and even looks again.

The Bible says that lust is one of the most dangerous problems we confront. The author of James wrote:

> ...each person is tempted when he is lured and entices by his own desires (lusts). The desire (lust) when it has conceived gives birth to sin; and sin when it is full-grown brings froth death (destruction, our downfall) (1:14—15).

As far as Jesus was concerned, lust in any form, especially when it becomes attached to our God-given sexuality is deadly business He counseled his followers to avoid it at the most extreme cost He said:

> If your right eye causes you to sin, pluck it out and throw it away; it is better that you lose one of your members than that your whole body be thrown into hell. And if your right hand causes you to sin, cut it off, and throw it away; it is better that you lost one of your members than that your whole body go to hell (5:29-30).

Obviously Jesus did not mean for you to take his advice literally. After all, removing the offending eye or hand would not necessarily remove the sinful thought from your heart. His point was to underscore the necessity of taking drastic action in dealing with the lustful look and the adulterous thought. You can't nurse it and pamper it, flirt with it ad enjoy it because it will turn out to be your ruin. The only alternative is to ruthlessly root it out of your life!

It may cause you as much pain as a physical amputation. It may mean breaking off a relationship which has become meaningful to you, but which is detrimental to your marriage and family, or your spiritual well being. It may mean getting help for your addiction to sexually explicit pornographic materials. It may mean that you have to exercise more self-control and discipline over your thoughts and conversations. It may mean that you have to start running with a different crowd. But, ultimately it means that you will have to yield your whole life to the Lordship of Jesus Christ. It will mean that you must give him permission to renew your mind and control your thoughts. It will mean that you allow him to change the pattern of your conversations and your behavior. It will mean that you permit his power to change you and make you an entirely new and different person!

It may be the most painful thing you have ever experienced. The questions is: are you willing to endure it?

CALLING IT QUITS
Matthew 5:31-32

AFTER ANN LANDERS HAD SPENT 29 YEARS as a counselor to the American people, after receiving over 8 million letters, writing over 10,500 columns o marriage, sex, divorce, religion and almost every other imaginable topic, after being read by more than 70 million folks daily in over 1,000 newspapers, she announced one day several years ago that after 36 years of marriage, she and her husband were calling it quits—they were getting divorced. She answered the unspoken question in the column: **How did it happen that something so good for so long didn't last forever?** Said she, "The lady with all the answers doesn't know the answer to this one." Ann Landers' experience reminds us of a basic truth: there are no perfect people, no perfect marriages. But, is that reason enough to call it quits in a marriage?

A Hollywood celebrity recently ended her 12-year marriage. She explained to one writer: "We got married when I was 23 and that's just too young. I'm not that woman anymore." Let's face it—nobody is the same person she was 12 years ago! In fact, we're told that mot people married for 20 years or more have altered over 50% of their values, personality, characteristics, and vocational plans. But, is that reason enough to call it quits in a marriage?

Let's fact it—with every passing day, the odds seem to be stacked more and more against the survival of marriage and family. This is not a marriage-friendly world any longer. The issues facing today's marriages and families are tougher than they've ever been, and they're pulling husband and wives apart.

Christians are not immune to the pressures that impact all people. Many of you have worked through, or at least, attempted to work through the death of your marriage. Frankly, it's been the hardest thing you've ever been through. And, it was made even more difficult by Christian friends and family, pastors and other ministers who roundly condemned you for your unwillingness to stick it out.

Some of you are thinking about calling it quits right now. You honestly don't know what to do. If you are a Christian, two of the biggest issues you face are how god will feel about you if you call it quits in your marriage and what the Bible really teaches about divorce. That's what this sermon is about. It's also the issue addressed by Jesus in this portion of the Sermon on the Mount, as well as on other occasions. The frequency of the divorce question in the New Testament indicates that we obviously have not changed much in the last 2,000 years. The issue that troubles us today was a "hot potato" even then.

Let's begin with a study of an additional passage in the Gospel of Matthew. Since we have already read form Matthew 5, let's look at Matthew's second account of Jesus' teaching on divorce. Pharisees came to Jesus with murder on their minds and deceit in their hearts. They hoped to "trip him up" and completely discredit him with the crowds in a discussion about divorce. "Is it lawful," they asked, "for a man to put away, that is, to divorce his wife for any cause?" (v. 3)

Jesus referred them to the teaching of Moses on which, you will recall, they were experts. In Deuteronomy 24:1-5, Moses stated that a man who divorced his wife must give her a written statement certifying that she was, in fact, divorced. Then, she was free to marry again. That's when the certificate became useful; it certified that she was not an adulteress but had been legally released from her previous marriage.

Moses' law also stipulated the grounds for divorce. A man could divorce his wife if he "found some uncleanness in her" (Deuteronomy 24:1). But, what exactly did it mean? During the New Testament era, there were two primary schools of though concerning the meaning of the phrase. The great Rabbi Shammai held a strict interpretation: the only acceptable grounds for divorce was adultery. On the other hand, Rabbi Hillel interpreted the same phrase very broadly. A man could divorce his wife for almost any reason at all, even if she burned his toast or failed to comb her hair the way he preferred it. He could even divorce her even if he found another woman he thought was more beautiful. Naturally, the second opinion was most appealing to the general male population. The Pharisees wanted Jesus to side with one of the two prevailing opinions.

He, however, shifted the focus from what Moses wrote to what God intended (vs. 4-6). He went back before Moses to creation and quoted from Genesis.

From the beginning of creation, male and female He made the; for this cause shall a man leave his father and mother and cleave to his wife…. What therefore God has joined together let no man put asunder (1:27; 2:24).

Jesus pointed out that Moses' teaching was not intended to encourage or even permit divorce. Rather, it was a concession to the sinfulness and stubbornness of the people. Moses established regulations regarding divorce to keep a bad situation from getting worse. The, he added the clincher:

> I tell you that anyone who divorces his wife, except on the grounds of marital infidelity...(v. 9).

Apparently, his won disciples agreed with the view popular among most of the man. Their reaction was somewhat surprising. Essentially they said, "Well, if it's that hard to get out of, it's probably better to never get married" (v. 10). You may be surprised at Jesus' response. For all practical purposes he agreed with them (vs. 11-12).

Mark apparently reports the same incident, although his version of what Jesus said differs form Matthew's, particularly on one essential point (10:1-12). The variation creates something of a dilemma. Did Jesus say, as Matthew reports, that divorce is all right, if your spouse has committed adultery or if you're the innocent party? Or did Jesus say, as Mark reports, that there are no grounds for divorce ever that what God has joined together no one should ever tear apart? (vs. 11-12)

If you take every verse of scripture literally, you have a tremendous problem with this teaching. You are forced to decide for one Gospel's account over another.

However I think there is a far better way to let the Bible be our guide than to use it as a means of pitting us against one another. But, before I give you what I think is the Christ like approach to the question for divorce and remarriage, I want to look at one other section of teaching.

To get the full New Testament picture on divorce and remarriage, we must consider the Apostle Paul's words in 1 Corinthians 7. Apparently, in light of Paul's teaching that the coming of the Lord was very near some wondered it they should even get married. Paul tells them that it is best not to marry. However, t they must, in order to meet their physical and emotional needs marriage is the only appropriate context in which Christians fulfill those needs. The Apostle Paul did not condone a man and woman living together as husband and wife <u>unless </u>the two of them are, in fact, husband and wife.

Then, in verses 1—11,Paul states what he believes is a clear and direct word from God. He writes:

A wife must not separate from her husband.
But if she does, she must remain unmarried
or else be reconciled to her husband. And a
husband must not divorce his wife.

In verse 19 he likewise indicates that divorce is not an option for two Christians. Their marriage may be broken only by death.

In contrast to this word from God, Paul states a personal opinion in verses 12—15. He says that if a Christian has an unbelieving spouse, and the spouse is willing to stay with the Christian the Christian ought no leave, that is, separate or divorce the unbeliever. He's talking about people who become Christians after they get married. However, if the unbelieving spouse decides to leave, that is, to call it quits in the marriage, the Christian should not try to stop it. In verse 39, he says that a widow may remarry if she marries a Christian.

So, what do we make of the Apostle Paul's teaching? At least four principles seem clear. First there should be no divorce among Christians. Second if Christians do call it quits, they should remain unmarried or be reconciled to each other. Third, if you are a Christian and you have an unbelieving spouse who is willing to live with you, you should not initiate any attempt to dissolve the marriage. However, if they want to leave, you are under no obligation to hold the marriage together. Finally, the underlying principle to all of this is that God has called His people to peace. Obviously, Pau's thinking is tempered by his strong conviction that the end was very near (vs. 26,29).

Is it possible to put all of this together in some coherent way? Is it possible to arrive a some understanding of a New Testament teaching on divorce and remarriage? The answer is year and no.

If you really want to know the biblical teaching regarding divorce and remarriage, you must be content to settle for principles based upon the Word of God. It that's what you want, this is what you will find.

First, God intention in marriage is one man and one woman together for life. Divorce is breaking of God's intention for marriage and as such, it is a sin. However, it is not a sin in a category all by itself. Nor is divorce an unforgivable sin. All of us sin. To make any one sin so hug and unforgivable that it ruins our lives every after is to make that sin bigger and more powerful than our God. Furthermore, I dare say that people who remain legally married in a living hell, although emotionally and spiritually divorced for year, sin more than those who, after sincere and prayerful efforts, failed in a marriage and divorced.

Second, to build a view of divorce on Matthew's exception for adultery smacks of legalism and ignores the plain teaching of Jesus in Mark's gospel. Furthermore, I find the attitude of some ministers that they will remarry divorce persons only if they are "the innocent party" to be very legalistic. It smacks of the attitude of the Pharisees.

Frankly, I have never seen in any divorce situation one spouse totally innocent and the other completely guilty.

Third, we have the words of Jesus on this matter recorded only in the context of controversy. Paul's words are advice given to a terribly confused church in a time when the Apostle felt that Jesus was definitely coming back in a matter of years if not months. We do not have all that Jesus may have said on this matter. It is possible to get the letter of the law and miss the spirit of the mater if we nail our view of divorce and remarriage on any one verse, or any one passage.

Fourth, we must consider Jesus' actions along with His words. Jesus forgave sinners. God wants His child to be happy and fulfilled. Jesus is more for you than He is against divorce! Therefore, to say that once divorced, you can never remarry is legalistic and harsh. It certainly does not reflect the spirit of Jesus in dealing with people. Perhaps the most appropriate teaching on this subject is His forgiveness of the woman caught in adultery I John 8. His treatment of sinners leads me to say that God throws out neither His holy intention nor His sinful children. What is clear is that Jesus wants those who believe I Him to live happy, fulfilled lives I commitment to Him.

Fifth, in light of the full teaching of Jesus I am, ministers must determine if they are willing to perform marriage ceremonies for divorced persons who are

Christians. Have they recognized that divorce is a breaking of God's intention and have laid this matter before the Lord in repentance? Has enough time to work through the grief and guilt associated with divorce passed before remarriage? God wastes nothing that happens to us and even from the ruins of a failed marriage there are lessons to learn. After a sufficient period of time, and remarriage is considered, a Christian ought to marry only another Christian, asking forgiveness for past failures, seeking the blessing of God upon the second marriage, and inviting Jesus to be Lord over the family circle.

Finally, in light of the full teaching of the New Testament, ministers must be intentionally committed to restoring a profound sense of sacredness and renew a deeper respect for the institution of Christian marriage. Ministers should prayerfully reserve the right to perform only those weddings where both bride and groom are Christians. That does not mean that both must be members of the same denomination. However both should be able to give witness of a personal relationship with God through His Son, Jesus Christ. Furthermore, ministers reserve the right to refuse to perform weddings for couples who are living together outside marriage. This is a clear violation of kingdom morality. If the couple is sexually active before marriage, ministers reserve the right to require of the couple a commitment of celibacy until after the wedding.

Human beings are sinners. All of us fall short of God's intention in many areas of our lives. Divorce adultery, and premarital sexual relationships clearly violate God's will for His people. However, none of those sins is unforgivable. Still, God has neither abandoned His intention for marriage nor His sinful child. He wishes for us all and works so that we may all have happy and fulfilled lives of faith. It is with this understanding that First Baptist Church and its ministers renew our commitment to extend God's grace and redemption to all those who are willing to allow Him to be a part of their life, a meaningful part of their marriage and family circle.

FICTION ADDICTION
Matthew 5:33-37

DO YOU REMEMBER WHEN MAJOR BABY food manufacturer admitted that it's 100% pure apple juice was just a colored sugar water with only a minimal amount of apple flavoring added?

Do you remember when substandard "counterfeits" were sold as high-test metal bolts used to build airplanes, creating the potential for massive loss of life?

Do you remember the revelations that major discount chains were offering inferior merchandise stamped with the brand name of quality products?

Do you remember a few years ago, when a relatively new tranquilizer was implicated in the deaths of over a hundred hospital patients? In the wake of the news, a representative of the pharmaceutical company even joked that they had expected to make $40 million with the new product line, "but if we had known how potent it was, we would have projected $80 million instead."[7]

And you certainly haven't forgotten the recent scandal involving one of the national television news organizations, have you? Apparently, a story wasn't spectacular enough. So, after another vehicle was rigged with minor explosives to make certain it burst into flames after colliding with another car, the incident was staged again for the cameras.

Unfortunately, lying and deceit are much too commonplace in our society. Candy bar wrappers twice the size of the candy bar; plastic toys that have no chance of surviving a few hours of play; advertisements that ignore a product's faults and exaggerate its quality. We are outraged by it all. And we agree, I'm certain, that corporations and politicians, public figures, news organizations, and those responsible for the car and well-being of other persons ought to be held to the strictest standards of honesty and integrity. When it comes to public morality, we expect consistent truthfulness.

But, tell me something: can we have honesty in the public arena if we don't also insist on it in the private sector – in the everyday business we conduct, in our home and marriage, in the classroom and the church, and in our

---

[7] Sheila Murray Bethel, <u>Making A Difference</u>. (New York: G.P. Putnam's Sons, 1990), p.76.

conversations with friends and competitors? How can we possibly demand truthfulness in the big issues which impact us all if we are not consistently credible in the little things which affect just one or two of us, or perhaps our family only?

Honesty doesn't happen easily, even among Christians. We all slip into little "white lies" and half-truths almost automatically. For what we consider the best of reasons – usually personal gain or advantage, or social or business convenience – we often compromise the truth without even blinking an eye.

Jerry White tells and interesting story about selling a 25 year old Volkswagen "bug." He knew that the car had both its good and bad points. But how much should he tell a prospective buyer? Should he only answer the questions the prospect asked? Or should he tell everything he knew? He decided that he had to tell all that he knew.

"The horn needs to be fixed... You will probably need to get new brakes before the next inspection comes around... The backup lights don't work... The wiper motor may be burned out." But there were some good points also. The engine had recently been rebuilt. The front end had just been replaced. Even as he said those things to the prospective buyer, the man looked at him with a quizzical squint-eye, as if to say: "Yeah, sure. And what aren't you telling me?"

The first person to look at it bought the car, however. They went to the tax office together to complete the bill of sale. Before they went in, the buyer suggested, "Now put down that I paid you $300 for the car." The problem is that he actually paid $500 for it. Jerry White said, "I really wouldn't feel right doing that since I'm a Christian. That would be wrong." The other guy said, "Well, I'm a Christian, too. I just hate to pay any taxes that I don't have to pay." Inwardly, Jerry White what the man was asking. And he was certainly sympathetic about the tax bill. But in the end, he couldn't compromise his commitment to honesty and truthfulness for a mere $12 tax saving. Did he lose the sale? No. But much more importantly, he did not compromise his integrity either."[8]

That puts into perspective the concern and focus of this sermon. That is precisely what this section of the Sermon on the Mount is about. Even in the New Testament era, lying and deceit, cheating and dishonesty were widespread – even among God's people. Clever, intricate little ways had been devised by which one person could easily mislead another. By using words which even had religious connotations, a person could say or promise one thing but mean something else entirely. It was hardly possible, even in the time of our Lord's earthly ministry –

---

[8] Jerry White, <u>Honesty, Morality, and Conscience</u>. (Colorado Springs: NavPress, Inc., 1985), p. 53.

to take the word of any person, even one of God's own people –at face value. Tell me: what's gone wrong when you can't believe even a Christian? What's happened when even God's people are not trustworthy - when even Christians can't be counted on to keep their word, or to dot he right thing? But fat more important than that: is it possible that you and I can become completely honest people in a deceitful, dishonest world?

I believe that we can. I also believe that the Apostle Paul helps us move in that direction with some very wise counsel he originally gave to some Ephesian Christians. He wrote:

> Let me say this, ... speaking for the Lord: live no longer as the unsaved do, for they are blinded and confused. Their closed hearts are full of darkness; they are far away from the life of God because they have shut their minds against Him, and they cannot understand His ways. They don't care anymore about right and wrong and have given themselves over to impure ways. They stop at nothing, being driven by their evil minds and reckless lusts. But that isn't the way Christ taught you. If you have really heard His voice and learned from Him the

truths concerning Himself, then throw off your old evil nature – the old you that was a partner in your evil ways – rotten through and through, full of lust and sham. Now your attitudes and thoughts must all be constantly changing for the better... You must be a new and different person, holy and good. Clothe yourself with this new nature. Stop lying to each other; tell the truth, for we are parts of each other and when we lie to each other we are hurting ourselves. (4:17-25, TLB)

The passage describes three things that Christians can do to overcome the increasing pressures of our world to re-define and compromise the qualities of honesty, truthfulness, and integrity. The first thing the Apostle Paul suggests is to learn what the truth looks like. He wrote: "If you have really heard his voice and learned from him the truths..." (v.21) God is the source of truth and Jesus reveals that truth. Do you recall his words when he said to his closest followers: "I am the way, the truth, and the life?" (John 14:6)

It's terribly tempting in the kind of environment where we live to compare our actions to those of everyone else. With enough practice at it, we are soon able where we live to compare our actions to those of everyone else. With enough practice at it, we are soon able – and without much effort at all – to find someone who always makes us look good. There's always someone who is a little worse, a little more deceptive, a little more clever and conniving, than we are. And when we find them, it really relieves us of a great deal of guilt because we're not nearly as bad or dishonest as are they. The fact is: compared to then, we look pretty good. But the truth is: when we do that, we're practicing the worst and most dangerous form of self-deception.

Stuart Briscoe tells an interesting story from his childhood which helps underscore the damage that kind of self-deception inflicts upon us. He grew up in little town in England whose sole source of livelihood was iron and ore mining. The miners stacked up all the waste from the mines in slag banks, like mountains. Many of the little houses perched right at the bottom of the slag banks only rarely saw the light of day. Once, he said, a little lady did her laundry and hung it out in the late afternoon. As she did so, she noticed how lily white the laundry looked against the backdrop of the huge slag banks. She felt good that everything was so clean.

During the night, however, it snowed in that little mining town. When she went out the next morning to gather her laundry, she could hardly believe how yellow it looked. Nothing had happened to soil the laundry. It's just that when you hang it against a black slagheap, it always looks fantastic. But when you compare it to a bank of white snow, it looks dreadful![9]

If I compare myself to an inside-out, upside-down culture- one whose values are unclear or in constant upheaval – I'll always look pretty good. So will you. I really need to hold my life up against Jesus. He is the standard of truth – about God, about you and me, about life. When I do that, then I'll see things more clearly. I'll see the lies, the deception, the untruth in my motives and desires. And once I face the truth about myself, I can repent and be forgiven. I can receive a new power to help me stand against a deceptive world.

The second word of counsel from the Apostle Paul is to learn to love the truth. Just prior to his words quoted earlier, Paul had written:

> ... we will lovingly follow the truth at all times – speaking truly, dealing truly, living truly – and so become more and more in every way like Christ... (4:15, TLB)

---

[9] D. Stuart Briscoe, <u>Playing By The Rules</u>. (Old Tappan, New Jersey: Fleming H. Revell Company, 1986), pp. 159-160.

Think about his words. Some people try to hide the truth – and call it love. Others are so truthful they will destroy you with it, and they call that love. But speaking the truth in love is a fine balance which only comes when we begin to understand how unloving it is to maliciously deceive, mislead, or destroy or defame someone. I don't want to do that to someone I love. I want to build them up, not knock them down. Out of that desire, I love the truth and hate deception.

According to the Apostle Paul, lying undermines the trust which holds us together. (v. 25) Imagine what would happen if we couldn't trust anyone else. Imagine what the economic, financial, and legal system would be like. Imagine what would happen if all the rules, laws, and watchdogs, if the press and the politicians were allowed to do exactly what they wanted. Scrap everything else – all the rules and regulations, all the ethics codes, restrictions and safeguards. It's a free-for-all. Everybody can lie and cheat and deceive us as long as they can get away with it. But, what do you have when things are allowed to degenerate to that point? A society that collapses – inwardly and completely! That explains what happens to marriages and families, to businesses and relationships which are built upon lies. Dishonesty destroys people and societies.

The final word of counsel given by the Apostle Paul is to begin to live the truth. When Ted Williams was 40 years old and closing out his career with the Boston Red Sox, he suffered form a pinched nerve in his neck. "the thing was so bad," he later explained, "that I could hardly turn my head to look at the pitcher." ... For the first time in his career he batted under .300, hitting just .254 with 10 home runs. He was the highest salaried player in sports that year, making $125,000. The next year the Red Sox sent him the same contract.

"When I got it," he said, "I sent it back with a note. I told them I wouldn't sign it until they gave me the full pay cut allowed. I think it was 25 percent. My feeling was that I was always treated fairly by the Red Sox when it came to contracts. I never had any problem with them about money. Now they were offering me a contract I didn't deserve. And I wanted only what I deserved." Ted Williams cut his own salary by $31,250![10]

---

[10] Quoted by Jerry White, Ibid., p.15

What do you think about that? Was it honesty or foolishness? Would you have done the same thing, or anything similar to it? How far would you get in today's world if you lived like that? Are you **that** committed to truth-telling – not just about you, or the world, not just about politicians and/or competitors – it means that I have decided to recognize the truth about myself. And that is that hardest thing I will ever do!

It's not easy to live like that - to live at the level the Lord has called us to live, a level of righteousness which exceeds anything our world has seen before. But then, we don't have to do it all by ourselves either. His Spirit of Truth – is with us forever. He will help us learn the truth, love the truth, and live the truth in a world held hostage by the power of deception and dishonesty!

_____

A QUESTION OF FAIRNESS
Matthew 5:38-42

GOSH! I WISH JESUS HADN'T SAID some of the things that he said. Take the text, for example. It might be all right to turn the other cheek to a small child who can't hit very hard anyway. But, it won't work in a grown-up world where your enemy just might knock the daylights out of you. And what do you think about being nice to everybody, giving to those who ask of you, and lending to those who borrow from you? Is it really our Christian duty to shell out to the professional beggar? There are plenty of people who know how to spot the soft-hearts, and they'll prey on you as long as they can. And what about the guy who will take the shirt off your back? Are you supposed to let him have your undershirt, too? There are people out there who will use, abuse, and take advantage of you every way they can. With human nature being what it is, you can imagine what would happen if you actually tried to live by these principles.

Don't you agree that these particular words of Jesus must be among the most impractical and impossible that he ever spoke? Yet, if you really want to follow Jesus, sooner or later you have to do some hard thinking about what he said. That doesn't mean that you can isolate a verse – or a passage of scripture – and build a lifestyle around it. You must respect its context. You must try to understand its meaning, and compare it to the teaching of other texts. Here is a good rule of thumb: what God reveals in one part of scripture will never contradict what He reveals elsewhere in scripture.

In that light, let's look more closely at what Jesus actually says in this text. Like the four building blocks of teaching which precede this one, the starting point for the lesson is the Old Testament law. According to the Law, if one person harms another, "...you are to take life for life, eye for eye, tooth for tooth, hand for hand, foot for foot, wound for wound, bruise for bruise." (Exodus 21:23-25) In other words, your revenge toward the person who injures you is limited by the Law to the exact amount of your injury. You are permitted to get even, but no more.

Prior to the Law, you were free to use unlimited retaliation against your enemies. If someone knocked out one of your eyes, you were justified in knocking out both if his, if you could get to him. If an adversary knocked out one of your teeth, you could knock out his whole set, if you were able. It was the law of the jungle – every man for himself, "might makes right," and all that sort of stuff. If you possessed the power to inflict more injury than you received, you had the right to do so.

Obviously, the end result of that kind of reprisal is mutual self-destruction. Where does it all end? On the other hand, if the initial act of violence meets with revenge in precisely the same kind and degree - an eye for an eye and a tooth for a tooth – that will be the end of the matter. Anyone can see that's better than unlimited retaliation – especially if you're on the receiving end.

But Jesus felt that the righteousness of his followers ought to go beyond that. In ways apparent to the whole world, their righteousness ought to exceed what the Law prescribed and permitted. So, he proposed a better way to deal with the harsh inequities of life. He told his followers, "Never respond to the unfairness you suffer, or the injustice and evil inflicted upon you with the same kind of behavior." Then he gave them four examples of how they should respond in specific situations.

The first concerns a painful slap to the face. (v.39) Jesus is careful to state that it was the right cheek that was slapped – making it, for most of us, the most insulting and humiliating kind of slap. It was a back-of –the-hand slap. He said that if it happens to you, take definitive and immediate action. Do not defend yourself and do not slap back. Instead, turn the other cheek – nit defiantly, but deliberately and with dignity – to demonstrate that you have seized control of the situation. Not only is it the standard Jesus set, it is the standard he fulfilled. The Apostle Peter recalls that

> when they hurled their insults at him, he did not retaliate; when he suffered he made no threats. Instead, he entrusted himself to Him who judges justly. (1 Peter 2:23)

The second example concerns a lawsuit in which one person brings legal action against another, intending to literally "take the shirt off his back." (v. 40) What does Jesus say to do, if you are sued? Move to a higher level of responsiveness. Don't get down on his level. In fact, before you do that, let him have everything you own. Let me show you how strongly the Bible feels about Christians and lawsuits. Remember the rule of thumb: look for consistency in various passages of scripture. Well, in another passage, the Apostle Paul insists that Christians ought to choose to be wronged than to enter litigation with another Christian. (1 Corinthians 6:7-8)

His third example refers to the Roman army's practice of commandeering civilians. (v.41) An ordinary soldier could legally command a civilian to help him. It

89

didn't matter if the civilian was busy with something else very important. For example, the soldier could force any citizen to carry his baggage for up to one mile. Anyone would resent such an order, be out done by it, and angered. Jesus, however, suggests a way to turn around the whole experience.

For example, allowing someone to backhand you – and get away with it; permitting someone to take the shirt off your back –without putting up any resistance; and submitting without argument to one who takes advantage of you does little or no good to either of you. The fact is: it harms the one who does it and the one who submits to it. But from Jesus' perspective, it's the other cheek, it's everything else along with the shirt off your back, and it's the second mile which turns everything around. Passive resistance reveals nothing but weakness. Active resistance, however, reveals pure strength. And it's that which tips the scale in favor of righteousness and good will. When someone will take everything I have, and I offer it to him without resistance; when he demands that I go a mile and I go another willingly, I have show his exploitation for what it is. The injustice has stopped with me because I refuse to perpetuate it.

The final example requires cheerful lending and willing giving. (v. 42) The issue is not the wisdom or foolishness of lending money to everyone who comes along. The burden of this verse is consistent with the ones before it; there is a better way to respond to those who take advantage of you. There is a way to turn an unfair and unjust situation to the advantage of your adversary as well as your own.

All four examples —although extreme and perhaps even a bit absurd —vividly demonstrate the radical demands of the kingdom of God. When it comes to the business of everyday living, kingdom citizens must take an approach radically different from everyone else in the world. Tell me: how do you typically respond to insult and humiliation, to lawsuit and coercion? Do you determine to get even, to fight tooth and nail, to fight fire with fire, to play as dirty and rough as the next guy? Do you make up your mind to teach them a lesson, to give them a dose of their own medicine? What's your reaction to an annoying and bothersome beggar or a borrowing neighbor? Do you get angry and put out? Do you try to get even? Are you bitter, cynical, and skeptical? Are you calloused and insensitive?

A Christian's response must never be determined by pride, nor by concern for personal convenience or inconvenience, nor by an insistence upon protecting his or her own rights, nor even by an appraisal of the advantage to be gained by a particular behavior. A Christian responds by the light of his or her relationship with God through Jesus Christ.

Will it work — putting a life together with little or no concern about being taken advantage of? Tell me, have you ever heard of Carl Sewell? He sells cars in Dallas — Cadillacs and Hyundais, Chevrolets, and Lexuses. In 1968, he did $10 million in business and last year, he did more than $250 million. His customer satisfaction scores are among the highest in his industry. How does he do it?

Listen to what he says. "Let's say it's five in the morning and you're leaving for work, and you discover that you have a flat... You call the showroom, and the policeman will phone the service technician on call 0 somebody is available 24 hours a day, every day — and he'll drive over... and take care of you... The technician will put your spare on —and, ...won't charge you for it —and you'll be on your way." He goes on to say: "The biggest problem we have... is that customers forget, or don't believe, we'll take care of them no matter what... We want them to call. They're our customers and we want to take care of them...Can the people who do call take advantage of us? Sure, but that doesn't happen often."[11]

Would you buy a car from that man? Sure, you would. And if the attitude Jesus describes in the text works

---

[11] Carl Sewell, Customers For Life. (New York: Doubleday Currency, 1990), p.15.

for Carl Sewell – and his primary concern is to make a profit – why wouldn't it work for you? The reason it seems so hard is because it goes completely against what comes so naturally to us. An unprovoked attack automatically prompts resentment and retaliation.

One of my favorite stories is about a practical joke Mickey Mantle pulled on his New York Yankee teammate, Billy Martin – one that backfired in Mantle's face. Mickey Mantle often hunted on the ranch of a friend in Texas. He took Billy Martin along on one of his hunting adventures. When they got to the ranch house, Billy waited in the truck while Mantle went inside to tell the rancher they had arrived.

The rancher asked a favor. His favorite old mule was at the point of death and needed to be put out of its misery. The rancher just couldn't bring himself to do it, so he asked if Mickey would be willing to shoot the mule for him. When Mantle came out of the ranch house, he slammed the screen door, stormed over to the truck, got his rifle and said," That sorry so-and-so told us to get off his property and never to come back. But before I leave, I'm gonna' kill his favorite old mule." Mantle marched into the barn and in just a moment, a shot rang out. Before he could get back to his truck, though, a shotgun blast also rang out. When he emerged from the barn , Billy Martin was standing over the carcass of a dead cow, smoking gun in hand. Martin said, "You know, I got so mad about what your friend told you that I shot his cow!" That's what comes naturally to most of us.

Let me tell you another story. For six years following their marriage, she loved and encouraged her husband and supported him financially. She deferred her own education, neglected her social life, and postponed having the children she wanted so badly so that she and her husband could build their dream.

Today, he's a successful doctor with a successful practice- a thousand miles from where she lives alone in a small apartment. Even before he finished his M.D. degree, he had an extended affair with another woman and took her with him to another state where he served his internship.

His wife? They're divorced now and she's saddled with the debt from their broken marriage. She can't afford to go back to school and can't force him to pay the court-ordered settlement even though he now has a six-figure income. She's bitter, and trapped by feelings of anger and betrayal. She wants to put him behind her, but her hatred is all-consuming.

She's a good, caring, conscientious person who has tried to do what's right. In return, she was used, betrayed, and tossed aside. What does God expect her to do? He doesn't expect her to be her former husband's doormat –

nor any other man's, for that matter. But neither does he expect her to allow her husband's mistreatment and abuse to shape the rest of her life. God is prepared to heal her broken spirit, to put together her broken dreams, and to strengthen and restore her bruised and fragile ego

What does she have to do? She has to let go of her hurt and fear, her natural inclination to wish him the worst life can offer. She has to turn loose of her anger, her bitterness and resentment. She has to accept God's forgiveness and learn to channel His grace even in the direction of the one who deliberately devastated her life. In doing so, she breaks his power over her and turns her life over to God who will never misuse or abandon her.

Some years ago, a young professional baseball player prided himself on being a really good hitter. He knew he could make it in the majors if he just had a chance.

For several years he bounced around the minor leagues. Toward the end of one season, however, the major league parent team called him up. They were in the thick of a heated pennant race and needed help. Day after day went by, the rookie was itching to bat to show them what he could do. But they kept him on the bench.

Finally one day, the manager called him to pinch-hit. It was a crucial game – last inning, score tied, and a runner on first base. This was his bug moment! He stepped in to the batter's box glanced toward the third base coach for his sign and couldn't believe his eyes! They wanted him to sacrifice – to make an out on purpose to advance the batter to second base, hoping that the next batter could bring him home.

The rookie ignored the signal. Instead, he took three hefty swings and struck out. When he got back to the dugout, the red-faced manager chewed him out. "What's the matter with you, son? We wanted you to sacrifice. Didn't you see the sign?"

"Sir, I saw the signal," said the young ball player. "I saw it, but I didn't think you meant it!"

On page after page of scripture, God tells us what He wants us to do – how He wants us to live –and how we're to respond when life is unfair, or we've been hurt and taken advantage of. Granted, this teaching won't work if you try to make it the basis of law and order in society. Nor does He expect you to walk away if your wife and children are threatened or, others are being abused. It couldn't be any clearer than it is. This is what He expects you to do if you are hurt and humiliated. And if He says it, He means it. You can always count on that.

GETTING RID OF YOUR ENEMIES,
ONCE AND FOR ALL
Matthew 5:43-48

I SAW A CARTOON RECENTLY IN WHICH a man appealed earnestly to the Almighty. "God," he said, "strike my worst enemy with lightening." In the second panel, the man was suddenly struck by a huge bolt from heaven. In the third panel, he picked himself up and said, "God, perhaps, I should re-phrase that."

The cartoon depicts what many of us consider the most effective way to deal with our enemies: destroy them as utterly as possible. The Pharisees certainly felt that that was the way to treat an enemy. What's more, they were sure that God felt the same way about His enemies, especially sinners. "There is joy in heaven," they used to say, "when a sinner is obliterated from the face of the earth." But, that's not exactly the way Jesus put it. His perspective was that "there is rejoicing in the presence of the angels of God over one sinner who repents." (Luke 15:10)

The truth is, there are fundamental differences between the righteousness of the Pharisees and what Jesus expects of His followers. The text draws to a close that portion of the Sermon on the Mount in which Jesus illustrates how kingdom righteousness differs from – and exceeds- pharisaical, self-righteousness. In Matthew 5, the six occasions of the words, "You have heard that it was said...", clearly refer to the teaching of the Pharisees, which might or might not accurately reflect Old Testament instruction.

For instance, verse 43 reads: "You have heard that it was said, 'Love your neighbor and hate your enemy.'" The Old Testament clearly instructs God's people to love their neighbor. (Leviticus 19:18) However, nowhere does it encourage God's people to hate their enemy. To arrive at that interpretation, one has to "play games" with the scripture. One has to take a clear teaching and twist its meaning for one's own purposes. That is precisely what the Pharisees did. They took the word "neighbor" in its most exclusive sense. "We are to love only our neighbors," they reasoned. "That is what the Law demands. But since it does not mention how we are to treat our enemy, we are free to hate them."

Jesus, however, imposes a different, much more difficult standard. He demands that we love our enemies. All of us have them. According to Matthew, they're the people who "persecute" us, who make life really difficult for us. According to Luke (6:27-28), they're the ones who mistreat and curse us – the ones who run us down to our friends and talk about us to people we don't even know. They're the ones who walk by us and never speak, the people who look down their noses at us. They are not abstract, faceless personalities. Enemies are real people we run into everyday. We know them by name – and mostly, we don't like them!

It would be much easier had Jesus told us to just love our friends, or to make certain that we love and care for our families. But His concept of love is far more radical and uncompromising than our own. For Him, love is more than caring for those whom we feel responsible because of blood kinship. It's even more that being concerned about those toward whom we have some obligation because we are daily thrown together in the work place. For Jesus, love is more than nurturing a relationship with one with whom we have chosen to be friends. Jesus demands that we love those we don't even like.

Does love make any real difference? I heard about a high school football team that was losing 28-0 at half-time. When they came back after the half, they looked like a different ball club. With five touchdowns and an awesome defense in the second half, they won the game 35-28. What made the difference was what the coach told them in the locker room at half-time. He said, "Guys, if you lose this game, I'll still love you. And if you lose this game, your mothers will still love you. But fellows, if you lose this game, I'm not sure that your girlfriends will still love you." Love always makes a difference and often, much more than we realize.

Jesus requires that we express our love by praying for our enemies. How do you pray for your enemy? Do you pray that they be forgiven - or punished? Do you pray that God redeem them – or obliterate them? It's my understanding that when you pray for another person, you take that person into God's presence, stand beside them, and speak to God on their behalf. In the act of prayer, you do for them what they are unable – or unwilling – to do for themselves. The more difficult they are, the more sincerely you pray for them. Why? Because as long as you stand with them in the presence of God, neither their hatefulness nor their insults will hurt or overcome you. Taking someone to God in prayer, being unwilling to stand with them in God's presence, is the supreme act of love!

It can be transforming to pray. I have a friend who's in sales. Not long ago, he had a falling-out with an associate over a client. After that, they didn't speak to each other for a very long time, even though they passed each other's desk every day.

One day in church, as he prayed for forgiveness and the ability to forgive others, my friend started thinking, "There was no question in my mind who was in the wrong," he said. "George was wrong for taking my client away from me and collecting the commission. But it's not right for us not to be speaking either. I had to so something. So, I asked God to help me with George. On Monday afternoon, I worked up my courage and went over to his desk. 'You know. George, you used to tell me about the trouble your wife is having with arthritis. I've been wondering how she's getting along.'"

"George looked shocked at first, but then words began to tumble out. They'd been to three specialists in the past year. She was a little better. He said, "Thanks for asking." As we talked, he told me about taking a walk with his wife the night before. They had gone two blocks before she had to turn back. And among other things, he said that he was too quick with his tongue and often did things he didn't really mean to do. Although he didn't come right out and say so, I knew that was George's way of apologizing."

"And the next morning when he came by my desk, he said, just like he used to, "Good Morning, Bob!" And I said, just like I used to, "Good Morning, George!"

It's only natural to wonder where this sort of response to your enemies will get you. Will it make any difference at all? Will it make you feel differently toward them? Will it make your enemies treat you any better? Will they ever apologize and admit that they were wrong? I wish I could tell you that every situation would work out exactly like my friend's experience. However, since I can't guarantee that, I want to explain as clearly as possible the promises that Jesus does make in this passage.

The truth is: He didn't tell his followers to love their enemies because it would or would not work. Actually, it probably never even occurred to him to raise the issue of practicality. If you think only in the short term – if you think only about today, tomorrow, next week or even next month- it may not get you anywhere at all. But, if you think in terms of eternity, Jesus gives you a word of assurance and encouragement. His promise is this: if you will love your enemies, go out of the way to do good things to and for them; if you praise them when they run you down; and, if you pray for them, "you will be sons (and daughters) of your Father in heaven." (v.45)

It's quite evident from the sunshine and the rain that God does not limit His love to only those who love and obey Him. Being what He is and acting as He does, God can't help loving everybody, regardless of what they are and how they act. It's only natural to hope that a child will pick up some of his or her father's most positive traits. It's normal to expect that some of the positive characteristics of the father will also become second nature to his child. It's supposed to be the same with God's children. Their behavior and attitude must not be determined by how their enemies treat them, even if they abuse them. Their response must be determined instead by their relationship to their Father. Hatred – even toward those who hate you – is an outright denial of your relationship to God!

But, there's one more thing. One of the most difficult verses in scripture is Matthew 5:48. It reads: "Be perfect... as your heavenly Father is perfect." At first glance, it's hard to swallow and difficult to accept. Never would we even remotely connect ourselves with perfection. We're too vividly aware of all our imperfections. They're much too glaring to admit.

But the word "perfect" doesn't mean moral perfection, nor does it refer to something beyond the realm of possibility for us. The word used here actually means grown-up, adult, complete, and mature, as opposed to petty, childish, and immature. Essentially then, this passage is a call to grow up – especially in our relationships with other people. The basic demand is that we stop acting so childish and being so self-centered.

At the height of the Cold War, a frightening incident took place at Kennedy Airport in New York. Just after the Russian invasion of Afghanistan, a plane carrying

Soviet ambassador Dobrynin was coming in for a landing. Suddenly his plane vanished from the radar screen in the control tower. The blip representing the plane, along with all the data showing its identity, altitude and speed mysteriously disappeared.

Fortunately, one of the air-traffic control supervisors walked by, saw the information vanish, and quickly took charge. He brought the plane in safely. However, in the confusion, it was brought in at the wrong altitude and through the wrong air space. Amazingly, no other planes were in its flight path and disaster was averted.

The FBI and FAA investigation revealed that an air-traffic controller, angry at the Russians, deliberately wiped the plane off the radar screen, hoping it would crash. Apparently, he had no concern about the damage such an incident would inflict upon already tense Soviet-American relations. It was entirely childish and thoughtless. What's more, it makes you wonder how many lives have been lost and how much harm has been done, by childish and immature people who don't know what to do with their enemies?[12]

Someone said once, "So far in the history of the world, there has never been enough mature people in the

---

[12] James W. Moore, Seizing the Moment. (Nashville: Abingdon Press, 1988), p. 65.

right places." That is perhaps on our world's greatest problems. Rather than pay the price for maturity in our relationships, we too quickly resort to childish, immature, and petty responses.

During the Civil War, General Whiting was known for his jealousy of General Robert E. Lee. He spread many vicious and slanderous rumors against him. The time came when General Lee had an opportunity to settle the score. President Jefferson Davis was considering Whiting for a key promotion and he asked Lee what he thought of Whiting. Without hesitation, Robert E. Lee commended his adversary in the most complimentary ways. Every officer was shocked. After the interview, one of them asked Lee if he had forgotten all the unkind and untrue things Whiting had spread about him. Lee responded, "I understood that the President wanted my opinion of Whiting, not his opinion of me." That was the mature response.

A friend of Clara Barton, the founder of the American Red Cross, once reminded her of an especially cruel thing that someone had done to her years before. Clara Barton, however, seemed not to recall it at all. "Don't you recall it?" pressed the friend. "You must remember it." "Oh no, I can't," said Miss Barton. "I distinctly remember forgetting it." That was the mature response.

As you may know, Paige Patterson is one of two architects of the "conservative resurgence" in our denomination. Last year, Patterson was named President of the Southeastern Baptist Theological Seminary in Wake Forest. He and Mrs. Patterson wished to join a local church. However, the Pastor suggested that their membership would be disruptive since members of the local church generally found themselves in opposite sides of the theological/political spectrum. The Pattersons then requested Watchcare membership, allowing them to remain members of First Baptist, Dallas. But by a vote of 16-1, Wake Forest's deacons denied the request.

What did it accomplish to deny membership in a local church to a seminary's first family? Michael Brooks, Pastor of the First Baptist Church, Selma. Alabama, recently wrote an insightful column in his church newsletter concerning the incident. He wrote:

> ..."Moderates" have talked for 14 years about the need for diversity and tolerance in the SBC. Shouldn't this attitude extend to the local church? Must we all think alike to worship and work together?

> The church missed an opportunity for dialogue and understanding. Both sides

might've gained insights and appreciation for each other.

I can see it now. At a church fellowship, a deacon with coffee and donut says. 'Paige, we liked Southwestern the way it was. Why did you feel it needed changing?" Dialogue, and maybe friendship, begins. ....an office Patterson opposes for women. He thinks, "Well, this seems to work here. Maybe I need to re-think my opposition."

But a golden opportunity was forfeited. The headlines could've been different: "Pattersons Join (Local Church) – Conciliatory Gesture Opens Way to Healing, SBC Leaders Say."

That would have been the mature thing to do. What's more, I think it's exactly what Jesus hoped for when He gave this lesson: followers who will act like their heavenly Father, instead of petty, pouting, self-centered and spoiled children! God, help us all to grow up!

HOW TO BE A CHRISTIAN WITHOUT BEING RELIGIOUS
Matthew 6:1-18

IN HIS NEWEST AND PERHAPS, most provocative book entitled *A World Waiting To Be Born*, Scott Peck describes a full-page advertisement which appeared in *USA Today* on January 29, 1990. Tiny print in the lower left corner identified the advertiser as Dun and Bradstreet, a large financial analysis firm specializing in rating credit risks. Other than that, the entire page was devoted to four brief sentences in very large type. This is how it read:

> I'M 30,000 FEET OVER NEBRASKA AND THE GUY NEXT TO ME SOUNDS LIKE A PROSPECT.
>
> I FIGURE I'LL BUY HIM A DRINK, BUT FIRST I EXCUSE MYSELF AND GO TO THE PHONE.

I CALL D&B (i.e., Dun and Bradstreet) FOR HIS COMPANY"S CREDIT RATING. THREE MINUTES LATER I'M BACK IN MY SEAT BUYING A BEER FOR MY NEW BEST FRIEND.[13]

Like it or not, that's the kind of world we live in: one where people pretend to be your best friend for all the wrong and completely self-serving reasons. It's a tactic some business people regularly use to enlarge their client base. It's a strategy others master to hurdle all the obstacles on the way up the social ladder. Even children have learned that relationships with certain other children are the easiest way to make the team, to be elected to the squad, or to get a date. It's just the kind of world we live in: one where it's practically impossible to tell who's sincere and who's just pretending.

I suppose it's really been that way for a very long time. It was obviously the issue that Jesus raised in this portion of the Sermon on the Mount. When he said, "Be careful not to do your acts of righteousness before men, to be seen by them," (v.1) he addressed this whole issue of why we act as we do and whom we are trying to impress.

---

[13] M. Scott Peck, M.D., <u>A World Waiting To Be Born.</u> (New York: Bantam Books, 1993) p.3.

Since it remains such a crucial issue for us even in 1993, let me set it in its context so that you can understand precisely what he meant.

First, understand that Jesus did not say that you should do nothing in front of others. He had already told his followers that they were the light of the world. Therefore, it was their duty to shine **before others** in such a way that the Father would be glorified because of them and the things they did. (Matthew 5:14-16) It would seem then, that he wanted them to do everything out in the open. After all, like it or not, most of what we do gets out anyhow, doesn't it? Neither our deeds nor our motives are kept secret for very long. People always speculate and second-guess, if not outright gossip, about what we do and why we do it. So, Jesus said, "Just be careful. Since they are going to talk about you anyway, just be certain that they only have good things to say."

In the second place, even though our lives are out in the open, what we do and how we live should not be motivated primarily by our desire to win other people's approval or to earn their admiration, applause, or congratulations. Let's face it: all of us are susceptible to flattery. When someone congratulates us for some accomplishment or success, or even agrees with some comment we made, it tends to go to our head. Once our egos are inflated, it becomes nearly impossible to ever get beyond our sense of self-importance.

Jesus reminds us that Christians do good things – righteous deeds –for the Father, who seeks the common good of all His children, rather than the exaltation of any one of them. To illustrate what he means, he sites three examples which specifically cover the whole range of human religious activity.

First, he addresses the issue of giving to help the needy. (vs. 1-4) Some only give if and when they are sure that others will know or find out about it. In the New Testament era, contributions to the needy were placed in large, metal receptacles located near the doorways of the Temple. Some brought their gifts only in coins – the more, the better. That would insure that when they poured their offering into the receptacle everyone would know about it because of the noise.

Then, Jesus addresses the issue of praying.(vs. 5-15) Most devout people pray several times during the day. In Jesus' day, there were specified times of prayer at approximately nine, noon, and three o'clock. However, instead of praying unpretentiously in their homes, or bowing their heads discreetly and praying silently in public, some arranged to be at the busiest intersections of the city at times of prayer. That way, they could literally stop traffic as they lifted their eyes and hands toward heaven, and loudly recite their prayer.

Finally, Jesus spoke to the matter of fasting. (vs. 16-18) That was an impressive thing to do –to go for an entire day without anything to eat – and to do it for religious reasons. Jewish law prescribed only one obligatory fast on the Day of Atonement. But people who were concerned that others know about their deep devotion also fasted on Mondays and Thursdays. Those were the principle market days in Jerusalem, so the city was literally packed with people. Those who fasted powdered their faces to make themselves look pale and gaunt. They dressed in clothing that marked them as being in pious mourning, thus drawing attention to themselves.

With perceptive insight, Jesus exposed the charade. The things they did were not done for God. They were intended only for the sake of a little attention, to earn a few admiring looks, and an occasional flattering remark.

In the past several years, John Trent and Gary Smalley have become best-selling authors in the Christian market. In one of their most recent books, John described a period of time during his childhood. He wrote:

> When my brothers and I were toddlers, my
> dad still lived at home – at least he slept

there. He would work all day and then go out with his buddies at night. Sundays, however, were an exception. Back in the early fifties, many people in Phoenix took a stroll down Central Avenue after church on Sunday afternoons.

All the nice shops were downtown at that time, and Central was the place to bump into all your friends and neighbors. Dad would be there too, pushing us twins in the stroller and leading our older brother by the hand. We would be all dressed up in our cutest clothes. Dad in his best suit. For a couple of hours, we would stroll up and down old Central. Dad smiling, waving, and greeting people.

Why the Sunday devotion to the family? Frankly, it was good for business. As an insurance agent, Dad thought it would help him make contacts if people saw him as a devoted family man with cute little kids. The rest of the week, however, he didn't want any responsibility for us at all.

My dad wanted two images, and he only kept the public one to enhance business. He thought that showing off...would bring him clients. But since there was no inner character to sustain the image, it soon collapsed. Within a few months, he gave up trying to maintain appearances and left the family for good.[14]

That's what this passage is all about – keeping up appearances that have no substance – pretending to be something that you're really not – maintaining two images: one for the public and one for your eyes only! Your children know when you're playing that game. Certainly, your wife knows. Surely, you must know that the Lord knows about it, too – don't you? Don't you ever wonder what He thinks about it – all this pretending, play-acting, and charade?

Well, you don't have to wonder because Jesus once told a story that dramatically reveals his attitude toward it. (Luke 18:9-14) Two men went to the temple to pray. One was a Pharisee and the other was a tax collector. Neither was very well liked. On the surface, people admired the

---

[14] Gary Smalley and John Trent, The Hidden Value of A Man, (Colorado Springs, Colorado: Focus on the Family, 1992), pp.126-127.

Pharisees. They were respectable enough, but it's hard to like someone who's always looking at you disapprovingly and condescendingly. The tax collectors fared no better. No one likes tax agents. They never have.

When these men prayed, the Pharisee prayed about himself. He thanked God that the world was full of people whom he wasn't like – and he named some of them. He was thankful to be able to say that he was better than extortioners, adulterers, the unjust, and of course, the tax collector. What made him better was the impressive record he had compiled: he fasted, he prayed, and gave regularly to the needy.

Meanwhile, in the far corner of the temple, the tax collector prayed. He was so deeply aware of his own sinfulness that he wouldn't even lift his eyes toward heaven – and he prayed for mercy. He had absolutely no claim to worthiness. If God's mercy was not broad enough to include him, he was doomed – and he knew it!

Jesus said that God heard the prayer of the tax collector and ignored the pretension of the Pharisee. The government agent want home justified, right with God. The religious man didn't. Why? Jesus said: "...Everyone who exalts himself will be humbled, and he who humbles himself will be exalted." (Luke 18:14)

Tell me: whom are you most like in that story? I think that most of us tend to identify with the humble man who confessed that he didn't deserve anything. We admire humility, a virtue that frankly, doesn't come easy to most of us – except when we read about these two men. We don't like the Pharisee. So we customarily read, teach, and preach the story from the point of view of the tax collector.

But I don't believe that there's much in that story for us if we look at it from that perspective. Luke recalls that Jesus originally told it for the benefit of people "…who were confident of their own righteousness and looked down on everybody else." (18:9) Honestly, I believe that more of us are like the Pharisee than the tax collector.

For instance, we often congratulate ourselves for the values we hold, the standards we cherish, the kind of life we live. We don't do it in church and certainly not in public prayer. We do so when we read the newspaper, or watch television talk shows – especially **Oprah, Donahue**, and others of that sort – or the evening news. That's when we're most likely to shake our heads in disgust and despair. That's when we tend to thank God that we are who we are – and that we are quite unlike the perverts and criminals parade across the screen! That's when we privately congratulate ourselves and think the world would be a lot better place if only more people were just like us.

Don't we talk and think like that? Don't we, honestly? And doesn't it honestly sound like the Pharisee in Jesus' story?

True worship of God – genuine prayer, authentic spiritual sincerity – makes you humble, not proud. Religion tends to make us proud. In fact, you don't even have to have a lot of religion to make you feel superior to others. It's just human nature that when most of us compare ourselves to other folks, we come out looking pretty good. Except for periods of depression, we all tend to see ourselves with a less critical eye and to be more conscious of someone else's faults than their achievements.

It's true. Frankly, in lots of ways, we **are** better off, more moral and civil, than lots of others. But God doesn't judge us against others. He never tells us to be at least as good as the next person and better than some. He demands instead that we become like Him! Even if we use our best behavior as the measure, we all come in last when compared to God!

So, let's stop pretending. Let's quit playing. More of us are in danger of the Pharisee's sins than those of the tax collector. We are not guilty of heinous crimes and perverted behavior. We have never "ripped off" another human being in our life. We are among our community's most respected and honest citizens. We are all of that – and more. Yet, we still may be shut off completely from

God. You see, self-righteousness holds out precious little hope that we will ever experience the grace of God. For one thing, it's difficult to believe that we need His grace if we also believe that we're such upright people.

That's why Jesus tells us to be careful with this "religion thing." Religion can do strange things to people. It can make you think that you're perfectly all right – even without God in your life. But the gospel is rooted in God's grace. And the gospel reminds us that although none of us deserves it, God reaches out in Christ and offers hope to us all!

"Be careful," Jesus said. "If you ever plan to get to heaven, you had better be more concerned about what God thinks than what your neighbor thinks. For that matter, what He thinks is even more important than what you realize about yourself."

I wonder: what **is** the real truth about you? Is it what you believe- and what you want others to believe about you – or is it what God knows? We both know the answer to that, don't we?

THE MEASURE OF YOUR TREASURE
Matthew 6:19-24

"ONE MAN'S TRASH IS ANOTHER man's treasure," the old saying goes. Homer and Langley Collyer dramatically illustrated its truth. They were sons of a respected New York doctor. Both had earned college degrees. In fact, Homer had studied at Columbia University to become an attorney. When old Dr. Collyer died in the early part of this century, his sons inherited the family fortune and estate. The two men –both bachelors – were financially "set for life/"

But the Collyer brothers chose a peculiar lifestyle, one not at all consistent with the material status their inheritance gave them. They lived in almost total seclusion. They boarded up the windows of their house and padlocked the doors. All their utilities – including water – were shut off. No one was ever seen coming or going from the house. In fact, from the outside it appeared empty.

Though the Collyer family had been quite prominent, almost no one in New York society remember

Homer and Langley Collyer by the time World War II ended. They had been almost completely forgotten.

Then, on March 21, 1947, police received an anonymous tip that a man had died inside the boarded up house. Unable to force their way in through the front door, the authorities entered the house through a second-story window. Inside, they found Homer Collyer's corpse on a bed. He had died clutching the February 22, 1920, issue of the Jewish Morning Journal, even though he had been blind for years prior to that. The macabre scene was set against an equally grotesque backdrop.

It seems that the brothers were collectors. They collected everything – especially junk. Their house was crammed full of broken machinery, auto parts, boxes, appliances, folding chairs, musical instruments, rags, assorted odds and ends, and bundles old newspapers. Virtually all of it was worthless. An enormous mountain of debris blocked the front door. Investigators were forced to continue using the upstairs window for weeks while excavators worked to clear a path to the door.

Nearly three weeks after they first entered the house, as workmen were still hauling away heaps of refuse, someone made a grisly discovery. Langley Collyer's body was buried beneath a pile of rubbish some six feet away form where Homer had died. Langley had been crushed to death in a crude booby trap he had built to protect his fool's fortune from intruders and would-be robbers.

More than 140 tons of garbage was eventually removed from the Collyer house. No one ever learned why the brothers stockpiled their pathetic treasure. One old friend of the family may have offered some insight, however, when he recalled that Langley once said that he was saving newspapers so that Homer could catch up on his reading if he ever re-gained his sight.[15]

The Collyer brothers are a tragic but fitting parable of the way many people choose to live. Although their inheritance was more than adequate to meet all their needs for a lifetime, they lived in unnecessary, self-imposed deprivation. Neglecting the abundant resources that were rightfully theirs to enjoy, Homer and Langley instead turned their home into a squalid dump. Spurning their father's sumptuous legacy, they binged – and overdosed –instead on the scraps of the world. Everyone else's trash was their treasure – and they died protecting it!

Too many people still live that way – accumulating and harboring relatively worthless treasure while ignoring the generous resources and lasting inheritance of their heavenly Father. Jesus was concerned about our

---

[15] John McArhur, "Treasure or Trash?" <u>Preaching</u>, Volume VII, Number 3, November – December, 1991, p.12.

relationship to things and the disproportionate value we place upon them. In fact, it is an issue He addressed frequently during his ministry. In his teaching, Jesus offers his followers a heavenly perspective on worldly treasures. Then he warns us of the dangers of yielding to worldly pressures. Finally, He reminds us of God's eternal provision which money cannot buy.

First, Jesus offers us a new, heavenly perspective toward earthly treasures. (vs. 19-23) The truth is that many of us waste our lives collecting litter – fleeting wealth that can be stolen or lost, plundered or squandered. But from the perspective of eternity, all of it is practically worthless. None of it offers any lasting benefit whatsoever. Essentially, we forfeit treasure for trash.

The reason we make such foolish choices is simply because we do not have a clear perspective on the true and lasting value of things. In the text, Jesus said:

> The eye is the lamp of the body. If your eyes are good, your whole body will be full of light. But if your eyes are bad, your whole body will be full of darkness. If then the light within you is darkness, how great is that darkness! (vs. 22-23)

The metaphor really is quite simple. The eyes are the "windows" through which we see the world. If the windows are clear and clean – if the eyes are healthy and good – we ought to be able to see everything clearly. We ought to be able to find our way without difficulty. However, if our eyes are weak and our vision blurred – if we have a "lazy" or wandering eye and are unable to focus both eyes in the same direction or on the same object – we are headed for certain disaster!

It's apparent, however, that Jesus was talking about developing a soundly spiritual perspective on life, not merely taking care of our physical eyesight. He had already spoken of the difference between earthly and heavenly treasures. Here he says that if the difference between the eternal and the earthly cannot be discerned – if your personal outlook on life is cloudy, unclear and distorted – unless you have a clear and unhindered perspective – your whole life will be chaotic.

One of the most talked about movies currently playing in theaters around the country is Indecent Proposals. (It's not a movie that I recommend you see and certainly not one that you should approve of your children seeing.) In the movie, Woody Harrelson and Demi Moore portray a struggling young married couple who can barely afford the things they want in life. Along comes the answer to all their problems in the person of Robert

Redford who offers the couple one million dollars for a single night with Demi Moore. Will she – the married woman – do it? Will he – her husband – permit it? That is what the movie is all about.

For me, however, the real intrigue has developed beyond the Hollywood set and outside the crowded theaters. I have been absolutely fascinated by the public discussion generated by the indecent proposal. Oprah recently devoted an entire show to the questions: "Would you sleep with a total stranger for one million dollars?" and "Would you permit your spouse to do so?" It's a proposition that's been talked about in restaurants and at bridge tables, in offices and even Sunday School classes.

Reportedly, part of the story's inspiration is based upon an actual conversation the famous playwright George Bernard Shaw once had with a beautiful woman who sat next to him at a dinner party. Supposedly, he asked her if she would sleep with him for the sum of 10,000 British pounds – an astronomical sum at the time. She replied, in the hypothetical spirit of the question that she might.

"Well, then would you do it for a sixpence?" – not much more than the change he may have had in his pocket at the time – he then asked.

"What kind of woman do you think I am?" she answered indignantly.

"We've already established what kind of woman you are," he replied. "We're merely haggling over your price now."

In a thousand different ways we all are tempted to "sell" ourselves everyday. We sacrifice a little of our integrity for a paltry increase in commission. We compromise our convictions - or abandon our principles altogether – to make or save a few extra dollars. We lie in order to secure some advantage or benefit, to reduce or avoid taxes or other fees altogether, and then live in the fear that someone will discover our deceitful secret and "turn us in." Is that the way God's People are really supposed to live?

In Jesus' view of life and things, it's not worth the trade-off. Don't you remember his penetrating question?

> What good is it for a man to gain the whole world, yet forfeit his soul? Or what can a man give in exchange for His soul? (Mark 8:36-37)

Jesus warns us also about the dangers of yielding to the world's pressures. (vs 24-25) We are a terribly confused culture. Our vision is blurred and distorted. We assess a monetary value upon practically everything and everyone. What's more, our natural instincts are exploited hundreds of times each day by the unrelenting pressures of a society saturated with a consumer –mentality. You do realize, don't you, that the dominant economic theory in America for the last forty years or so has not been capitalism and free enterprise, but consumerism – the notion that a progressively greater consumption of goods is somehow beneficial?

Do you know how it all got started? At the end of World War II, our country had the capacity to manufacture far greater amounts of products than people were buying. So, the American public had to be motivated to somehow buy more. That's when the giant advertising agencies began to emerge. That's when millions of dollars began to be invested in professional marketing strategies and campaigns. Furthermore, that also explains why, after only two or three years, we all began to "itch" for a new car. The ads on TV and radio and in the newspaper were good at making us believe that we need the new car when in reality, the one we have could likely have run for many thousand more miles.

Do you see what's happening to us? The slick ads and the subtle – and not-so-subtle pressures to buy, buy, buy and buy some more, catch out eye and distort our perspective on things. We are rendered virtually powerless within ourselves to resist the vigorous marketing campaigns with all their grandeur scenes, glitter, glitz, and grandiose promises. It's no wonder that we've lost sight of the eternal kingdom of God and forgotten the vast heavenly inheritance which is ours. What is the appeal of heaven and eternity alongside the best advertising money can buy? Our prolonged exposure to that kind of philosophy has made us self-indulgent and impatient people. Many of us – and more of our children – find it practically impossible to cope with life if every desire cannot be immediately fulfilled.

Jesus warns Christians that you cannot live long that way. Sooner or later, you will realize the impossibility of serving God and simultaneously worshipping at the altar of consumerism. It's another way of saying that we can love one or the other but not both. Either money and material goods own us – or God owns us. It can never even be a joint partnership between the two!

From Jesus' perspective, God's Word cannot thrive – indeed , it can't even survive – in a heart that's cluttered with the cares of the world. Do you remember the story he once told about the sower and the seed? (Luke 8:1-15) As the sower scattered the seed by hand, in broadcast fashion, it fell on a variety of soils. Some fell upon the tilled ground but some was also left exposed to the birds and the elements. Other seed even fell among the thorn bushes. It took root, eventually began to shoot up, but before long was choked out by the wild thorns.

In explaining the spiritual significance of the story to his disciples, Jesus said that the seed represents the gospel and the soil represents the various responses of persons to it. He said the seed which fell into the thorn bushes, it "..stands for those who hear, but as they go on their way they are choked by life's worries, riches and pleasures, and they do not mature." (v.14)

Many of us simply don't believe that has to happen to us. We sincerely believe that we are able to maintain a proper balance between the demands of the kingdom and the pressures of a materialistic, consumer driven world. Someone once said that, as a result, a whole new generation of Christians has come up believing that it is possible to "accept" Christ without forsaking the world. But when Christians are bogged down with debts – and some of you know what I mean – and when Christians are intent on getting in the race to accumulate the most material possessions – and others of you certainly know what I mean – the accompanying worry and anxiety leave little or no room at all for the claims of Christ and His sovereign presence. Jesus warns us of the danger of yielding to the world's pressures and its pleasures.

But in Jesus, God supplies our eternal provision – something money can never buy. Do you remember the wealthy young man who went to Jesus begging for security and peace of mind? (Mark 10:17ff) He desperately wanted confidence for his future – something his wealth had not given him. Jesus told him that in order to have what he wanted, he must first get rid of what he had. Jesus knew immediately that this man's attachment to his wealth was what was keeping him from finding joy in his relationship with God. So he offered the man freedom from his slavery to his possessions. But the man refused the offer.

I read about a man who stumbled upon a sunken treasure while on a scuba diving adventure. He marked its location precisely on his charts and started back to shore. However, his boat began taking on water and he had to abandon the vessel. So around his waist he tied a money belt containing the gold he had already discovered and the chart marking its location. But he was unable to make it all the way to shore with the extra weight around his waist. His only other choice was to leave it behind, which he wouldn't do. The man drowned with a money belt full of gold and the map to his treasure strapped to his body. Tell me, did he have the treasure – or did it have him?

Tell me: do you really own everything that's titled in your name – or are you it's slave? We are like the wealthy young man in Mark's gospel: we need to be free from our slavery to worldly values, from our false dependence on material security, from the deceptive measures of our own worth. Christians need to be free to love God and feel the joy of being loved by Him!

Jesus died and rose again to set us free. So, loosen your hold on worldly treasures. When you do, you'll find those empty hands filled with heavenly and eternal blessings!

WHY ARE YOU WORRIED?
Matthew 6:25-34

PERHAPS YOU HEARD ABOUT THE MAN who was a perpetual worrier. He worried about everything all the time! His family, friends, and work associates could hardly stand to be around him because of his constant worry. One day, however, one of his friends noticed him uncharacteristically bounding down the street. He was whistling and humming, wearing a huge smile and speaking to everyone he passed. He looked as if suddenly, he had no cares in the world. The friend was astounded and wondered what had come over him.

"What's happened to you?" the friend asked. "You look like a different person. You don't seem to have a worry in the world. I don't remember when I've seen a happier man than you seem to be."

"Things have changed," said the former worrier. "I haven't worried about anything for the past three months."

"How have you managed that?" pressed the friend. "Tell me your secret."

"Well, the truth is, I hired someone to do all my worrying for me."

The friend was intrigued. "Tell me," he said "how much does it cost to have someone worry for you?"

"A thousand dollars a week," the reformed worrier responded in a matter-of-fact way.

His friend was shocked. "A thousand dollars a week? Where do you come up with that kind of money?"

"I don't know," said the man, as he walked away humming and whistling again. "That's his worry."

At one time or another, all of us have wished for someone to take some of the worry-load off our shoulders. From what I recently discovered, most of us could use someone like that now. During the past two weeks, I conducted my own informal survey among a representative sampling of people in our church and community. Here's what I discovered.

More than seventy percent of the children I interviewed who are in fifth through eighth grades are worried about being separated from either one or both of their parents – either because of being "kidnapped," or because they worry that their parents might separate or divorce. More than sixty-five percent of high school students are worried about college – if they will have the grades to get in and what college they will attend. More than eighty percent of college students are worried about finding a job after graduation, and that they'll have to move back home if they don't.

A large majority of married men worry about losing their jobs and not being able to provide for their families. Most married women worry about the health and well being of their husband and children. Most single men and women worry about finding a lasting and loving relationship. Most senior adults worry that- in their advancing years and declining health – they'll become a burden to their family and friends.

Everybody seems to be worried about something. In fact, I believe that worry may be one of the crucial problems facing us today. It's certainly not a peripheral issue, one that we can put off dealing with while we address more significant concerns.

God is obviously interested in helping us deal with our worries. In the text, Jesus clearly states several practical principles for overcoming our tendencies toward worry and avoiding its destructive impact. He says first, that we should recognize that worry is a waste. Then, he challenges us to realize that we can live only one day at a time. And finally, he calls us to exercise our faith in God. Let's look more closely at what he says.

First, recognize that worry is a waste! No practical, positive benefit ever comes from worry. (vs. 25-27) There are simply some "givens" in life – some things that will never be any different. There are imperfect things – and people – that we have to learn how to accept and with which we must learn how to cope and co-exist. In reality, there are lots of things like that.

You can control your schedule. You can control your work habits and most of your personal actions and reactions. You can control your feelings toward others. You can even control your weight. Those are things you can change. They're things over which you have some measure of control. In fact, you ought to take charge of those things over which you have power and influence.

On the other hand, don't fret about things you can't change. For instance, you have no control over when or where you were born or the parents to whom you were born. You have nothing to say about your birth order. What's more, what can you do if you're unhappy with your height? Not one thing, right? Those are simply part of the "givens" of life, things about which you can do absolutely nothing. And mostly, you don't fret about them, do you? Because you know that it will do you no good!

If you've learned how to live with those "givens" and to make the best of them, there's hope that you can also learn how to accept the other unalterable facts of your life. You simply need to learn the difference between the things over which you have control and the things which you will never be able to change.

Are you familiar with the prayer used in Alcoholics Anonymous meetings? It was written by German theologian, Reinhold Niebuhr, and is more appropriately known as the "Prayer for Serenity." It reads like this:

O God, grant us the serenity to accept
What cannot be changed;
The courage to change what can be changed,
And the wisdom to know the difference.

No doubt, a large portion of your worry is about things and people over which you have no control and your worry will have absolutely no influence or impact. However, as long as you refuse to acknowledge that your worry will change nothing, you will remain captive to your anxiety.

Several years ago, a young, single mother became desperately frightened. During the day, she worried that burglars would break into her home while she was at work during the day and steal everything that belonged to her and her small children. At night, she worried that someone might break into her home and assault her and the children. Maybe it was because of so much TV violence, or news reports on increases in the crime rates, or rumors around town of break-ins – or a combination of all these factors. Whatever the reason, she became so obsessed that her fears mushroomed to paranoia. She installed heavy-duty, reinforced burglar bars on all her windows and doors.

Late one evening, she left her children asleep for a few minutes while she quickly ran to the grocery store only two blocks from her house. While she was gone, the house caught fire. Even though everyone worked frantically to get to the children, the security bars couldn't be removed in time. Tragically, both that mother and her children were trapped by her fears and worries but ultimately, her anxiety destroyed the children.

In a different sense and on a different level, your worries always cost you dearly. Jesus said, "Who of you by worrying can add a single hour to his life?" (v. 27) Yet, the reverse is true. The effects of worry can actually shorten your life span. Doctors report that eighty percent of stomach disorders are not organic, but functional. In fact, some say that most ills are caused by worry and fear.

Ironically, the word "worry" comes from an Anglo-Saxon root meaning "to strangle" or "to choke." Unfortunately, worry often lives up to its essential meaning. It suffocates our joy, chokes our confidence, and robs us of the kind of life which faith in God through Jesus promises to bring. When will we realize that there are no practical, positive benefits to be derived from our worry?

Next, Jesus challenges us to realize that we can live only one day at a time. (v. 34) Several years ago, the City Council of Jacksonville, Florida, considered purchasing a dramatic invention for each of its fire trucks, police cruisers, and other city-owned emergency vehicles. At a cost of $16,000 per unit, the gizmo would turn all the traffic lights green as the emergency vehicle approached an intersection. That would be a handy device for each of us to have on our waists, wouldn't it? As hectic and demanding as life has become, can you imagine having nothing but green lights all of your trip, throughout your life?

Obviously, that's a fantasy that will never come true. However, if we insist on compressing too much life in too short a period of time, our problem with worry will never be solved. Frankly, many of us try to live two or three days ahead of time – all the time. To complicate matters and add even more to that already overwhelming burden, we also drag around a great deal of the past –especially regrets, mistakes, and failures. Some way, somehow, we must learn that we can only effectively live one day at a time.

Do you remember what Jesus said? He said, "...do not worry about tomorrow, for tomorrow will worry about itself. Each day has enough trouble of its own." (v. 34)

A little boy couldn't help but notice that his father always brought work home with him from the office. Every night and weekend his dad shut himself up in his study to work. The father and son never had any time together any more. Finally, one day the boy asked his mother why his dad worked so much. She responded simply that he just wasn't able to get it all done at the office anymore. Perceptively, the little boy said, "Well, if he can't keep up, why don't they just put him in the slower group?"

The psalmist wrote, "This is the day that the Lord had made; let us rejoice in it." (118:24) It's a simple reminder that today is the only time you have. If you focus upon today – and only today – you're much more likely to be free of your worry and to have reason to celebrate and rejoice!

There's a story about a man who heard a noise in the middle of the night. He went downstairs to investigate and sure enough, found a burglar emptying the silver chest. He said to the man, "Stay right where you are. I want to get my wife. She's been expecting you for over twenty years."

It's probably the most serious obstacle to overcoming the worry in your life: worrying about what may happen tomorrow. If you think back to the results of my informal survey, most of the things you are worried about now are things that might happen in the future. In fact, most of the people who talk to me about personal issues talk about things that might be in their future. Listen. :"This is the day that the Lord has made." It is all you have. Pour everything you have into it. Make the most of it. It will soon be gone!

Finally, Jesus challenges us to exercise our faith in God. (vs. 28-33) Believe that God knows and cares about you and then give Him a chance to do something for you. A young man once boarded a crowded bus headed for the airport. There were no empty seats so he stood in the aisle immediately behind the driver. With all the starts and stops, the turns and swerves, the man had great difficulty maintaining his balance. He could only hold on to his large suitcase. The bus driver noticed how difficult the ride was for the passenger to he made a simple suggestion. "Sir, why don't you put your suitcase down and let the bus carry it for a while? You'll sure be able to hold on a lot better."

God knows the ride gets rough sometimes for all of us. He knows how difficult it is to stay balanced and hold on. That's why the Bible tells us to put all our cares and worries upon Him. He cares deeply for each of us. (1 Peter 5:7)

According to the Apostle Paul, there is a practical strategy for winning over worry. He wrote:

> Do not be anxious about anything, but in everything, by prayer and petition, with thanksgiving, present your requests to God. And the peace of God, which transcends all understanding, will guard your hearts and your minds in Christ Jesus. (Philippians 4:6-7)

In other words, overcoming worry can be divided in three basic stages. First, there's the premise: stop worrying. The there's something to practice: start praying. Finally, there's t promise: discover peace. The promise is there and available, b we must follow the first two steps in order for the third to occ We must stop worrying, exercise our faith in God through pray and be receptive to the gift of His peace.

There's just one more verse you must claim. Underline it your Bible. The prophet Isaiah wrote:

> You will guard and keep him in perfect and constant peace whose mind ...is stayed on You. (26:3, The Amplified Bible)

Whatever you choose to think about and to dwell upon will either produce – or dismiss- worry. Those who are overwhelmed by worry choose to focus their minds on negative thoughts and to anticipate the worst. But those whose mind and imagination is centered on God –what He has already done and will do for you –and the promises of Scripture, discover peace which transcends even the worst problems.

Fifty years ago, a man named Felix Powell sat down at his piano and played an old tune that he had written. It was tremendously popular during the critical, stressful days of World War I and had experienced a resurgence of popularity in World War II. He sang it again and again: "Pack up your troubles in your old kit bag and smile, smile, smile!"

This time, however, when he finished the song he went to his bedroom, took out a revolver, put a gun to his head and shot himself. Powell could write a song about troubles and worrying over them but he couldn't save himself.

Listen. It's not just words – all this talk today about worry. It's gospel, and that means that it's the truth. There is a peace which the world cannot give – and it's yours through your faith in Jesus Christ.

DON'T JUDGE ME TOO HARSHLY!
Matthew 7:1-6

A REPTILE FARM NEAR THE LAKE of the Ozarks has a most unusual exhibit. A long series of glass cages house some of the world's most dangerous and poisonous snakes and lizards. Tourists pass down the line looking at one after another of the deadly creatures. As they approach the last exhibit, a large sign announces: *"The Most Dangerous Animal In The World."* Most are surprised to see that the only thing in the cage is a mirror! When you look inside, all you see is yourself!

The message is clear: of all the creatures on earth, humans are the deadliest and most dangerous. Humans have the potential to do more damage than any other living thing. But we also have the potential for good. And that's what this portion of the Sermon on the Mount is all about. It's about what bad people do — as well as the good — and it's about our need to know the difference between the two.

In these few verses, Jesus addresses three simple concerns: the fact that we see so clearly the faults of others; secondly, we fail to see as clearly our own shortcomings; and finally, our need nonetheless, to develop a more discerning eye. Let's look at each concern more closely.

First, Jesus says that we see with perfect vision the faults of others(vs. 3-4). To a large extent, it's just one of the stages we all go through in growing up. One of our basic needs is to establish our own self worth and during adolescence, we become especially adept at doing that primarily by belittling others. Surely, you've noticed that teens spend an inordinate amount of time criticizing the behavior, tastes, and dress of almost everyone they know – including their parents and their siblings. You've probably also noticed that they can be especially brutal in the things they say and unusually cruel in the ways they treat those who don't measure up.

Unfortunately, some people never outgrow their need to behave that way. A man emerges from an all-day staff meeting or conference, and from his analysis, it was nothing more than an assembly of blithering idiots...with one exception, of course. Others seem to live under the compulsion to subject every person they meet to ruthless and destructive criticism. They're masters of snide and sarcastic comments. They take great delight in pointing out the faults of others. They rejoice when others fail. And if by chance, they can't find anything to criticize, they can always raise questions about another's motives or intentions.

All of us find it easy to point out the faults of others. We complain about our co-workers. We're quick to criticize elected officials, our favorite targets. We're adept at noticing the mistakes neighbors make in raising their children. Surely, Jesus had us in mind when He asked: *"Why do you look at the speck of sawdust in your brother's eye and pay no attention to the plank in your own eye? How can you say to you brother, 'Let me take the speck out of your eye,' when all the time there is a plank in your own eye"(vs. 3-4)?*

Why are we able to see so clearly the faults of others? Why are we so perceptive in seeing where someone else falls short? In our more honest moments we have to admit that there is no simple answer to these questions. We are a bundle of needs and a mixture of motives and consequently, a multitude of factors make us relate to people in the ways that we do.

One of the more obvious reasons is that pointing out the faults of others, we cut them down to our size. We just don't care at all for people who come across as too good, too noble, too high and mighty, or too successful. Too much of any good quality in someone else tends to pose a threat to our own self-image. Therefore, if we can chip away at their reputation – even the slightest bit – or, if we can cause someone else to lost just a little bit of their personal popularity or public respect – it'll keep them from out-distancing us by too much of a margin. It will keep us within striking range. Who knows? If they don't get too far ahead, maybe we will even catch up and move beyond them.

Sound trivial and trite? It does, doesn't it, especially when we talk about it so openly. But the fact remains: for most of us, life is measured by comparison to others. If someone else comes across as too good, we feel less adequate. If someone else is held in too high esteem, we feel diminished and unworthy. If someone else is more successful than we are, then in our estimation, there's less for us to achieve and acquire.

We deal with the dynamic by making certain that whatever flaws and shortcomings exist in another are magnified in the public eye. We have learned that we can make ourselves look good by choosing the right people as the basis for our comparison and by comparing our virtues to their flaws, our strengths to their weaknesses.

A second reason we judge others so harshly is that we seldom know all the facts and circumstances of their life. On the cross, Jesus prayed that God would forgive His executioners and torments because *"they do not know what they are doing"(Luke 23:34).* There were serious limits to their ability to comprehend all that God revealed of Himself and His purpose in Jesus.

Those responsible for His death acted, in large part, out of ignorance. That's not meant to imply that they were irresponsible and not to be blamed. The fact remains that their stubbornness and obstinacy contributed to their ignorance. They did not welcome or receive Him or His teaching because, as far as they were concerned, there was nothing *He* could teach *them*.

We don't like to admit it, but many of us are blood-kin to Jesus' harshest critics. Seldom do we take the time to learn about another's circumstances or situation before we pass judgment and condemn them. I admit that I am guilty.

When I pastured in Gravel Switch, Kentucky, during seminary, Tommy and Sylvia were members of the congregation. They were a childless couple who owned, and worked by themselves, a small dairy farm. In the first weeks I was there, it became apparent that Tommy couldn't stay awake for an entire worship service. Since he was a deacon, it didn't take long for my patience with him to wear very thin.

Eventually, it came time for the Orbersons to host Carol and me in their home for Sunday lunch. That's when I learned that Tommy suffered from chronic arthritis. He hadn't slept in a bed for several years. Most nights, he sat up in an old recliner, his arms hanging straight down by the side of the recliner through the night, his legs as high in the air as he could get them. He didn't sleep much at all in that old chair, but at least it relieved some of his pain.

Although I had expressed my frustration with Tommy's sleeping through the worship services to no one but Carol, Tommy and Sylvia apologized profusely to me on that Sunday. They explained why he slept through most of the services. After I listened, I understood. And I apologized to them and asked for the Father's forgiveness.

To tell you the truth, not a lot of dramatic things happened in that little church during the three years I was there. But one of my fondest memories that I still hold in my mind today, is Tommy sleeping through the sermon. And it never bothered me again after that first Sunday we sat down at the kitchen table in that little Kentucky farmhouse – the day I learned the *whole truth.*

Jesus was concerned about why we see co clearly the fault of others. But, He also observed that *we fail to see our own shortcoming as clearly as we should.* He said: *"You hypocrite, first take the plank out of your own eye, and then you will clearly to remove the speck from your brother's eye"(v.5).*

Why are we so blind to the fault within ourselves? Why are we so resistant to facing and admitting our own failures? *For one thing, we have this notion of ourselves as good and virtuous and upright people.* At least, we believe that we are as good as most people we know and better than some. A hard look at what we really are, what we have really done, where we have actually failed and inflicted pain upon others, may well shatter that image.

Everybody needs a positive self-image. What happens to that if we look too hard and take too seriously all the things in our lives for which we can be faulted? It just plain hurts to admit that we're selfish, or that people are turned off by our arrogance, or that friends and family stay out of our way because we're so opinionated, or out temper is so uncontrollable. Because it hurts to admit, we develop an amazing capacity not to see it.

Perhaps you heard about the wife who said to her husband one day, "You won't believe this, but our weekend guests stole our four best towels."

"Are you serious?" said the husband. "I guess some people are like that. They're just made that way, you can't trust 'em. By the way, which towels did they take?"

"The real fluffy white ones," the wife said. "The ones with Hyatt Regency written on them."

God calls us to complete transparency and honesty in all things, especially with regard to ourselves. There is some goodness and badness in all of us. The little rhyme is true: "There is so much good in the worst of us, and so much bad in the best of us, that it hardly behooves any of us to talk about the rest of us."

Unfortunately, unless our goodness is tempered with an awareness of the bad, the sinful and the frail that is also within us, our goodness can turn hard, brittle, and even cruel. Blindness to the reality of our own faults leads to an arrogance of our own spirit. And if we can believe what the Bible says about Jesus, self-righteousness was the least attractive of all the qualities found in people.

Why? Self-righteousness sharply limits the possibilities of strong and meaningful relationships with others. If we're always judging others for their faults, we have little capacity to understand them. If we have no awareness of our own weaknesses and shortcomings, we'll never have compassion for and patience with others who struggle with their faults. What's more, if we refuse to admit our own sinfulness, we will shut off ourselves entirely and eternally from any possibility of ever experiencing the grace of God! The end result of seeing clearly everyone else's shortcomings and denying our own is a lonely, tormenting existence.

That, however, raises the third issue. Our typical response to this warning from Jesus is to withhold any and all judgments in order to avoid being condemned. But notice that Jesus doesn't forbid all forms of judgment.

Rather, and this is His third concern, *Jesus urges His followers to understand the desperate need to develop a discerning eye.*

Jesus often called His disciples to exercise discernment in all aspects of life. Don't you remember? He warned them against false prophets. He told them to learn the difference between a sheepskin with a sheep in it and a wolf masquerading in a sheepskin. He told them that they should be able to judge a tree by its fruit. He denounced evil. He tried to arouse within them a more sensitive conscience, a surer power of evaluation between good and bad, and between something which only seemed to be good and something else which was truly good.

Go back to the text. Jesus said: *"Do not give dogs what is sacred; do not throw your pearls to pigs. If you do, they may trample them under their feet, and then turn and tear you to pieces"(v.6).*

Admittedly, it's a rather cryptic statement, one difficult to understand. But let me help you see what it means. Anyone who appreciate the value of beautiful jewels guards and protects them. You would certainly never deliberately throw a strand of priceless pearls to pigs. In the same way, when you truly appreciate the precious treasure of the gospel, you will not treat it as trash, nor will you allow anyone else to abuse it. Some things are clearly wrong for followers of Jesus. And sometimes, Christians get out of line completely. At times, out of our fear of appearing too judgmental, we takes those things too lightly, or overlook them completely. This passage is a call for Christians to take a stand.

Recently, a friend appealed to the first five verses of this text as his basis for the rejection of an examining and interview process for deacon candidates and other leaders in the church. "Who are we," he asked sincerely, "to set ourselves up as judge over anyone? None of us is worthy to do that." And, of course, he is right.

At the same time, it's also clear that Jesus does not mean for us to "mind our own business" and allow just any belief, any lifestyle, any doctrine pass itself off as Christian if, in fact, it stands in clear contradiction to everything for which He stood. Jesus knows that we ever become the kind of men and women that kingdom citizens should be, and if the church ever becomes all that He intends for it to become, we *must* become "judges" in some sense of the world, albeit very wise judges.

What our Lord condemns here is the impulse to stand in judgment *over* others. What He calls us to exercise in our judgments is mercy, not perfection. So, even if we were to begin to establish certain standards for leaders and members of the church, it doesn't have to be an exercise of self-righteousness. Instead, it can become a way of frankly stating that we believe that membership and leadership should be something that carries within them certain expectations.

We are not God and never will be. Only God is able to judge perfectly, because He alone is God, the judge of the whole earth. And according to His Word, one day He will judge each of us! When it's time, our only appeal will not be how we compared to someone else. Our only appeal will be to His mercy!

HAS THE GOLDEN RULE LOST
SOME OF ITS LUSTER?

Matthew 7:12

THE LATE SENATOR THOMAS HART BENTON was once asked about the most difficult part of being a United States Senator. He responded that, for him, the hardest thing was the frustrating fact that his constituents in Missouri had a "bad case of the simples"! That is, they tended to reduce all the complexities to neat little black-and-white simplicities. As a result, they expected quick solutions to every problem. They didn't seem to realize that the most meaningful and enduring accomplishments take time, effort, commitment, sacrifice, discipline, and perseverance.

We all tend to be that way to one degree or another – even in our personal faith experience. We want something simple and uncomplicated to believe in, to fall back on, and to build our life around. For many, that is the attraction of the Golden Rule. It's simple. It's short and easy to remember. It's practical and what's more, it represents decency and common sense.

Many believe that the Golden Rule is the essence of the Christian faith. Ask them if they're Christians and lots of folks will tell you, "Well, I believe in God and I try to live by the Golden Rule." For them, that proves undeniably that they are Christian. The fallacy is that nothing in this world is simple, if by simple we mean easy to grasp, prove, or even demonstrate. Nothing falls into that category – not even this word from Jesus!

In fact, the great tragedy associated with the Golden Rule is that, as "golden" as it is – as marvelous, wonderful, noble, high-sounding and beautiful as are these words from Jesus – most of us still do not understand the radical nature of what He demands. So, in this sermon I want to help clarify its meaning. I want to highlight three basic truths: first, practicing the Golden Rule does not require personal faith in Jesus; second, practicing the Golden Rule requires that we do something, not that we do nothing; and third, practicing the Golden Rule requires that we do something that we would really like for someone to do for us.

First, merely practicing the Golden Rule does not require faith in Jesus.. Twenty years before the birth of Christ, a Gentile skeptic approached two rabbis, Shammai and Hillel, and asked them mockingly if they could teach the whole law while standing on one foot. Everyone – including the Gentile – knew that the law of the Hebrew people filled numerous books – or scrolls, in that day. To read is all would take several days and nights. Shammai recognized the absurdity of the request and told the scoundrel to be on his way. Hillel, however, accepted the challenge and, as he stood on one foot, taught what he considered to be the whole law, "Do not unto others," he said. "what you would not have others do to you."[16] On another occasion, he reportedly expressed it with a slight variation. "What is hateful to you, do not do to your fellow creatures," he said. "This is the whole law. All else is explanation."[17] It's important that you understand that this was twenty years before the birth of Jesus and fifty years before he preached the Sermon on the Mount.

What's more, it's not only the Jewish and Christian faiths that teach the Golden Rule. For instance, several centuries before Jesus, Confucius said, "Do not unto others what you would not they should do unto you." Buddhist writings include the statement, "Hurt no others with that which pains yourself." Hinduism states, "Do

---

[16] Robert M. Holmes, Why Jesus Never Had Ulcers. (Nashville: Abington Press, 1986), p.25.
[17] D.A Carson, The Sermon on the Mount. (Grand Rapids, Michigan: Baker Book House, 1978), p.112.

naught to others which, if done to yourself, would cause you pain."

Obviously, the teaching we refer to as the Golden Rule – if taken by itself - does not belong exclusively to us Christians. Therefore, it only follows that simply practicing the Golden Rule is not evidence of a personal relationship with God through Jesus Christ. In fact, it could characterize practitioners of any number of religious faiths.

The Church of England's Archbishop William Temple, was getting dressed early one morning in a home where he had been an overnight guest. When he started down for breakfast, he heard his hostess singing enthusiastically, "Nearer My God To Thee." He was impressed that she would work at her menial chores while singing one of the great hymns of the faith and so, he spoke a word of appreciation to her. "Oh, yes," she replied, "That's the hymn I use for boiling the eggs – three verses for soft boiled and five for hard boiled."[18]

Things are not always as they seem, are they? Some people quote lots of scripture, others wear religious symbols as jewelry, insist on sending greeting cards containing only religious themes, sing lots of Christian songs, and plaster their cars' bumpers with stickers and tags which, they hope, will give certain impressions about

---

[18] Robert H. Spain, How To Stay Alive As Long As You Live. (Nashville, Dimensions for Living, 1992), p.135.

themselves. Hymns are great affirmations of our faith. Knowing and using scriptures are good. Religious symbols have always been as expression of our faith. But the question is: are these true marks of a real Christian, and only a Christian?

There is a story about a young man who studied music with the famous Pablo Casals. The student wanted very much to be a good musician and worked hard at doing everything correctly. One day he played a difficult piece for his teacher and was extremely pleased with how well it went. He was certain that he would hear an approving word from the maestro. However, instead of praising him, Casals said, "You are playing the notes, but not the music."[19]

In much that is touted as "Christian," the music is missing. Many "notes" are played in the right ways, but something is lacking. Just as there are imitation diamonds and works of art, so also there is much that claims to be Christian that does not have the stamp of Jesus upon it.

Don't misunderstand me. Obviously, the Golden Rule has the mark of Jesus all over it – especially in the way that He re-stated it. But it is also clear that Jesus did not say that merely praising – or even practicing - the principle gets anyone into heaven. He only said that

---

[19] Ibid. p. 134

behaving according to the teaching sums up the Law and the Prophets – meaning that it represents the basic kingdom principle of the kingdom of God. Frankly, no one can really practice the Golden Rule as Jesus re-stated it without first having experienced a radical, personal transformation by the power of God.

Why? The answer brings us to the second point: **namely, that practicing the Golden Rule in the power of Jesus Christ requires that we do something, not nothing!** Many people still have the notion that Christian faith is primarily expressed in terms of things a person does not do! And of course, there are some things that Christians should never do. Jesus made that perfectly clear. Yet, there is more to authentic Christianity than what a person does not do.

Did you recognize the one common characteristic shared by all the statements of the "golden rule principle" which pre-dated the birth of Jesus? Without exception, they were stated in a negative form. For instance, one said, "Do not do anything to anyone that you would not want them to do to you." Hillel said, "What is hateful to you, do not do to anyone else." Each of the others was similar.

Translating that to a practical, everyday perspective would result in attitudes like this. If you don't want to be bothered by your neighbors, then leave them alone. If you don't want to be robbed or have your home burglarized, then don't rob or burglarize someone else's home. If you don't enjoy being cursed or gossiped about, then don't curse or gossip about someone else. If you don't want to be hated, then don't hate others.

It's relatively easy for people like you and me to live by the Golden Rule then, isn't it? Frankly, given our nature and the kind of people we are, it really doesn't even represent much of a challenge for most of us. We're just not the kind of people who rob, burglarize, hate, interfere, and do mean and destructive things to others.

During the first quarter of the 1800's, near the end of Beethoven's life, some unknown musician made a small alteration in the construction of the harpsichord – a slight change which subsequently altered the whole development of western music. Before that, most of what we call piano music was composed for that instrument. But because of its design, the music itself was quite limited. The strings of a harpsichord are plucked by a small hook, producing a sound even in intensity and similar to that of a harp. In the change, the hook was replaced by a hammer, so that the string was struck rather than plucked. This minute alteration made all the difference because it increased the dynamic range of the instrument. Thus, the harpsichord became a piano. And the way was paved for the dramatic and thrilling compositions of Rachmaninoff,

Schubert, Brahms, Liszt, and Chopin. From that point on, the development of music revolved primarily around the piano.[20]

The story illustrates the radical nature of the change Jesus made in the Golden Rule simply by turning it around and putting it in a positive form. Suddenly, the Golden Rule became for more searching and demanding than it had ever been previously. In fact, it became an entirely new teaching – something which had never been said before. It represented a new attitude toward life and the responsibilities we have in life. It put everything in a new perspective.

It teaches us to live like this: if you want to be loved, then love others. If you like to receive things, then give to others. If you like to be appreciated, appreciate others. The way Jesus put it removes the restraints from life. Christians no longer live out of the fear of doing something wrong, or offending someone, and consequently, doing nothing positive in the world. Instead, they begin to live aggressively and generously, determined to be initiators of a new lifestyle –one that reflects the nature of God and His eternal kingdom.

---

[20] James Montgomery Boice, The Sermon on the Mount. (Grand Rapids, Michigan: Zondervan Publishing House, 1972), p.279.

Do you remember the three different parables Jesus used to describe the final judgment scene in Matthew 25? The chief difference between the good and the bad was the good had done something positive and the bad had not. Isn't it time that you understood that practicing the Golden Rule means doing something positive, not doing nothing at all?

In fact, **the third truth is this: practicing the Golden Rule in the power of Jesus Christ does require what we do things we would truly like for someone to do for us.** IT doesn't mean that we should do nice things for someone else because we subscribe to the philosophy, "what goes around comes around." When we think like that, our kindness becomes entirely self-serving. Then, the primary reason for doing something nice for someone else is the selfish wish that they will return the gesture and perhaps, be even more generous in their response.

Suppose one of your neighbors is constantly throwing parties and inviting people whom you would like to have as your friends. So, you throw a super-duper backyard barbeque and invite the whole neighborhood, being very careful to make certain that the neighbors from who you want a reciprocal invitation can attend. Have you followed the Golden Rule? Certainly, from one viewpoint you have. You've done for them precisely what you want them now to do for you.

But, from another perspective – and this one, far more important than your own – you've missed the point entirely! Do you honestly believe that that is how Jesus intended for us to interpret and apply the Golden Rule?

Some have suggested that another reliable guide in applying this principle is to put yourself in the other person's place. Once you've done that, then and there treat the other person as you would want someone to treat you. But how far can you take that? If you were a child and wanted everything that our children are always wanting, would you want to be refused? Following this word of advice would require that we give our children everything they desire and that we withhold nothing. And what about the convicted felon brought before the judge? Putting yourself in his place, you must realize that you would want to be pardoned and set free. So, why should the judge not free the prisoner?

Perhaps, the surest guideline I know for applying the Golden Rule is this. On those occasions when a neighbor, co-worker, competitor, in-law, or acquaintance receives good news, or is the beneficiary of an unexpected windfall and you are tempted to be envious or resentful, apply the Golden Rule. How will you know when those times arise? That's more obvious than you think. When you catch yourself thinking – and especially, when you are about to say – "Nobody ever did anything like that for me.

I sure wish someone would be that nice or generous to me." – then and there is the time to apply the Golden Rule. It's on the times like that that you'll discover how much like Jesus you have become.

Obviously, living by the Golden Rule day in and day out is not for those who want life simple and uncomplicated. Living the way Jesus intended us to live can clearly be accomplished only as we live in the same power and strength , and out of the overflow of the same kind of relationship He enjoyed with His heavenly Father. You can have that power and strength, you know. You can have that same kind of relationship with the Heavenly Father. It's entirely up to you!

A MULTIPLE- CHOICE TEST
Matthew 7:13-14

IN SOME PARTS OF THE WORLD, people stand in line for half and hour or more just to get a bowl or small bag full of cereal. What they're given is all that's available, so they take it gladly and go on their way. Here in America, you and I go into a supermarket and walk down gleaming aisles, totally in awe of the variety of cereals available to us. There are sugarcoated and candy-coated assortments and right next to them, fat free options. Some have to be heated, some must be eaten with milk, but many can be munched on right out of the box. Some are shredded, some flaky, others come in a variety of shapes. You could spend a half hour deciding which one to buy. In the end, you lose about the same amount of time as those who stand in line in other parts of the world just to get what's available. Our way – the American way – is certainly a lot more fun, isn't it?

At the same time, it's all these choices that's complicated life so much. The simple act of buying sneakers affords more that 1,000 styles form which to pick. Over 30,000 different software programs are available for the IBM PC user. The American car buyer must choose from more than 572 makes and models. Even toothpaste comes in 138 different varieties – tubes, dispensers, decorator colors, toothpaste for smokers, for folks with sensitive teeth, for coffee and tea drinkers, and for those with yellow teeth.

We live in a multiple-choice world. Gone are the days of Henry Ford who refused for years to offer customers different models and colors. His pronouncement that car buyers could have "any color they wanted as long as it is black" worked for awhile. But it won't work today. His company would never survive with that attitude. We want choices!

In fact, we demand so much diversity in the marketplace that it's carried over into every other area of life. As a result, the sheer number of options available to us is staggering – and to say the least, stressful! For instance, consider the mind-boggling diversity of today's job market. In just the past few years, the number of occupational and life choices has multiplied exponentially.

High school teachers and college students still sit around munching pizza and talking about what they're going to do with life. But the possibilities are more bewildering that ever. Instead of simply considering law, medicine, of business, they're discussing brand new fields. Now, they talk about computer programming, health care, research, non-profits, 1-800-Teach-America, even stand-up comedy. They consider teaching English abroad, international trade and banking, New Age Bodyworks (whatever that is), the Peace Corps, the Marine Corps, and a thousand other options. They even consider getting more than one degree – staying in school and remaining dependent upon parents longer – so that they can be qualified to pursue multiple careers. After all, they know that not all of them will get jobs as efficiently as they earn their degrees.

The possibilities are so overwhelming that surveys in college placement offices indicate that most students wish there were fewer choices available. It's certainly understandable. As long as you're actively considering doing sixteen different things, it's hard to feel like you're maturing, becoming more grounded, and resolving any of your life's significant issues. Our world is a multiple choice world and living in it any more is like taking a multiple-choice test every day. The pressure is almost unbearable.

So, let me give you three practical principles for preparing for the daily multiple-choice test. Principle number one: you can have practically anything you want, but not everything you want. On lots of ways, it's the most difficult principle. At some point, you must understand that making choices and commitments is essential to life and success.

Do you remember Olympic champion Mary Lou Retton? She wasn't born a classic gymnast. She wasn't naturally graceful, nor did she innately possess the movements of a ballet dancer. She was just a four feet nine inches tall, with a compact, muscular body. Frankly, she looked more like a sprinter than a potential gymnastics star.

But Mary Lou knew what she wanted and, at six years of age, she decided to pay the price. By the age of fourteen, she was West Virginia's State Gymnastics Champion – competing and winning in meets around the world. Still, she wanted to work harder, push further.

So, at the time when most teenagers are thinking about everything but commitment, Mary Lou made an enormous sacrifice. She left home and moved to Houston, into a home of a family she didn't know, just for the opportunity to train under one of the world's greatest, but most demanding, gymnastic coaches, Bela Karolyi.

While the other kids her age were watching TV, going to movies, hanging out with friends, and going on trips, she practiced four hours every day, seven days a week. Karolyi changed everything she had been doing for eight years, from the way she tumbled to the food she ate.

As the Olympic games drew closer, she worked out early, went to school, worked out late, and went to bed.

A grind? Sure. Fun? No way. So, why? Because winners work at doing things the rest of us won't even consider trying. Mary Lou may not have enjoyed the rigorous routine of it all, but she loved the sport, the challenge and the dream.

Just a few weeks before the summer games, her right knee suddenly locked. Fragments of torn cartilage broke loose and became wedged in the knee joint. But less than ten days after the arthroscopic surgery, Mary Lou was back in the gym for a full workout. There was no time to lose, only time to get ready to win. She hadn't prepared so hard for so many years to let it slip away from her. Her commitment – and the choice she had made when she was six years old – kept her going.

In her final event – the vault – Mary Lou needed a 9.95 – a near perfect - to tie the Romanian favorite for the gold medal. One writer described her effort this way: "She raced down the line, sprang off the vault, twisted at high altitude, and landed as still as a dropped bar of lead, yet as soft as a springtime butterfly."

Mary Lou Retton scored a perfect ten, something which had never been done by an American in Olympic competition. To the surprise and awe of spectators, officials, and participants, she went ahead and executed the optional second vault. Under the rules of the game, if she made a mistake, slipped, or was momentarily distracted, she could lose her first ten and forfeit it all. Incredibly, the result was the same – a perfect ten!

The only one not surprised was Mary Lou. She was ready to enter the winner's circle, because she had decided that out of all the things she could do, that was what she wanted most to do and she was willing to pay the price for it.[21]

Sometimes, I know, the price of success – whether you're talking about vocation, school, relationships, or even your spiritual journey – almost seems like paying the country's national debt all by yourself. It seems practically overwhelming when you consider the investment of time and effort, commitment and sacrifice required to achieve what you want. Too often, you want something, and want it badly – but you want it along with everything else – and you're not willing to give up everything else. And that's where the problems start!

People have always made that mistake with their lives. They dabble in everything and excel at nothing. They follow every whim, fad, and fashion of the day. They're always changing jobs, transferring from on college to another, moving from place to place. They never seem to

---

[21] Dennis Waitley, New Dynamics of Winning, NewYork: William Morrow and Company, Inc., 1993 pp.39-40.

be able to make choices: to choose one thing and to let go of everything else.

It was the issue Jesus addressed in the text. Obviously, he did not intend to explain to people how to become great gymnasts, or pianists, or artists, or scientists – even though his principles certainly holds true in those fields. Jesus described life- how to have it, and how to be happy and content with it. He warned people to stop gallivanting all over the world in the endless, futile search for cure-alls and end-alls for everything that ails us. He challenged people to stop wasting their life and opportunities and to realize that the one thing they want – life – can be theirs – but they have to be willing to give up everything else!

WOLVES IN SHEEP'S CLOTHING
Matthew 7:15-23

IT ALL STARTED OUT AS A SILLY JOKE but ended up as a startling lesson about the unbelievable gullibility of the American public. It happened last year, and it cam immediately on the heels of a television network's exposure of the shocking fraud imposed upon their faithful supporters by some of our nation's most prominent tele-evangelists. Two morning radio personalities in Dallas –the home of some of those exposed as frauds – spoofed the fund raising techniques of the evangelists charged. They pretended to be ministers in desperate need of raising emergency funds to keep their ministry alive. Several times during their show on several consecutive mornings, the disc jockeys aired their absurd and ridiculous appeals. They were confident that it was obvious to their listeners that it was all a hoax. But two weeks later, the station had to figure out how to stop the contributions that were pouring in and return the $20,000 they had already received from sincere, well-intentioned listeners who wanted to help the non-existent ministry survive.

There are lots of phonies "out there" and tragically, many of us are not able to recognize them. Most of us are extremely un-discerning about what we hear and in whom we believe. Politicians win elections because of it. Advertisers and manufacturers profiteer because of it. Newsmen mold public opinion because of it. The truth touches every area of life: you can't believe everything you hear. Even with regard to spiritual matters, we are often at the mercy of charismatic personalities. Frequently, we are victimized by their powerful, emotional appeals, and carried entirely away by their unsound and absurd doctrines. We should know better.

After all, the Bible repeatedly warns us about people like that. Jesus called them "wolves in sheep's clothing." The Apostle John referred to them as false prophets and deceivers. (1 John 4:1-4) In the first of two letters to a young minister named Timothy, the author warned that

> ...the Holy Spirit tells us clearly that in the last times some in the church will turn away from Christ and become eager followers of teachers with devil-inspired ideas. These teachers will tell lies with straight faces and

do it so often that their consciences won't even bother them. (1 Timothy 4:1-2, The Living Bible)

We live in those times now! People are increasingly sensitive to spiritual realities, more aware of personal spiritual needs, in search of more stable anchors for living, longing to know if there is some eternal purpose that will make sense of all the good and bad experiences, the joys and sorrows of life. As a result, there is a general willingness to listen to almost any and every explanation which sounds in the least bit "spiritual" or even remotely reasonable. We want someone to tell us about the meaning of life and we'll listen to anyone who claims that they can!

There's real danger in that kind of spiritual gullibility, however. You see, it makes a very big difference what and in whom you believe. Religion can be a good thing. But misdirected, it can be a very, very bad thing. Religion can produce a Moses, a Paul, a Mother Teresa, a John Wesley, or a Billy Graham. But it can also produce a David Koresh, a Jim Jones, or even a Charles Manson. When religious ideas are true, they save, heal, and make whole. When they are false, they crush, and destroy and devastate.

When I was in my first year of college, I had a good friend named David. He was one of those delightful characters who was always the life of the party. He was always grinning – always on top of the world. Everybody liked David. He was a friend to everybody. He was the guy – you know the type – who was forever broke, always bumming a quarter or a dollar off someone, but somehow nobody seemed to mind. He could walk into a room and everybody would soon be laughing and feeling good. He had a unique, happy, charismatic personality.

One day David got "religion." Unfortunately, it was the wrong kind. He changed completely – and immediately. Sadly, it was a change that was negative and debilitating. Within a few weeks, David became so sanctimonious that everybody felt uncomfortable around him. People started avoiding him. He didn't smile anymore. He rarely spoke – and when he did, it was with a very pious, condescending tone. He carried a Bible under his arm and constantly preached a negative religion, always laying it on in a holier-than –thou tone.

One day as we were sitting in the cafeteria, David came striding through very pompously, as though he were the perfect blend of John the Baptist, Jesus, Paul, and Billy Graham all rolled into one. Someone at the table said, "You know, I liked him a lot better before he got religion!' You know what that comment meant, don't you?

Don't misunderstand me. Obviously, I'm for religion. I've committed my life to it. But I'm also aware that the biggest problem Jesus had was with religious folks like my friend David. Religious people can be God-like, but when their motives get mixed up, when their thoughts become confused or self-serving, they may wind up nailing somebody to a cross. Good religion, on the other hand will open you up like a flower. It will make you bloom with new life. It will set you free. But bad religion will cause you to wither and die. It can make you narrow and unbending, negative, self-righteous, and closed-minded.

That's why the issue Jesus raised in the closing paragraphs of the Sermon on the Mount is so important. There are a lot of confusing religious ideas and spiritual appeals in our world today – all vying for our attention, all trying to win us over to their way of thinking, all claiming to be worthy of our loyalty. So, how do we tell the difference between good and bad religion?

Let me help you. Here are four basic qualities of good religion. You can probably think of come others. I simply want to plant some seed-thoughts which will grow in your mind long after this worship hour.

First, good religion keeps growing. It is open to the continuing revelation of the living God. David Koresh closed the book on truth. According to his followers, in twice-a-day preaching sessions, he impressed upon the

Branch Davidians that he alone understood the scriptures. Even though he changed his interpretations frequently, any who challenged or questioned him could be brutally punished.

Don't you see how wrong that is! A call to discipleship is a call to grow in the faith – to think, to stretch, to wonder, to probe, to love God with our minds, as well as our soul and spirit. That's why you need to be careful of any religion which shuts down thinking. Be careful of any teacher or preacher who says, "Here's what to believe. Learn this, believe this, accept this, and swallow this. Don't ask questions and don't bring up any new ideas!"

Second, good religion works in the world in daily life. Its power is not limited to the spiritual realm and the churchly arena. Good religion works **now**! It makes us better people **now**! Good religion is not merely an insurance policy for another day. Jesus came off the Mount of Transfiguration, walked right down into the valley, and healed an epileptic boy. (Mark 9:14ff) Good religion is not just something that dwells on the past or longs for the future. It is not focused entirely upon heaven. It works **now**, speaks to us **now**, makes a difference in life **now**!

I heard about a man who had been away from his home church for some years, involved in all kinds of shady practices and criminal activities. But when he came back to his home church and testimony-time came, he was ready.

He stood and said, "I'm so glad to be back home. It's true that I beat my wives – every one of them. It's also true that I deserted my children, that I stole and lied, got involved in some things that landed me in jail for several years. But I want you to know, brothers and sisters, that not once in all that time did I ever lose my religion!"

If your religious faith is nothing more than an insurance policy for heaven – if it has no effect on how you live and how you treat others **now** – then first of all, you are missing out on life. And second, you'd better check out your motivation. The Christian faith is good religion because it works in everyday life. It gives us a sense of personal partnership with God.

Third, good religion makes you more loving. In fact, this was Jesus' first test. For him, love was the measuring stick for good religion. For him, love was the most genuine, the most reliable, the most authentic sign of Christian discipleship. Do you remember how he put it in John 13:34-35? He said,

> A new commandment I give to you, that you love one another; even as I have loved you... By this all men will know that you are my disciples, if you love one another.

Now, if you have a religious experience and it makes you more loving, then, in my opinion, it is a valid experience. It's good religion. But if you have a religious experience that makes you narrow, or hateful, or critical, or judgmental, or negative, or holier-than-thou, then, in my opinion, that's bad news and bad religion. Parents, beware: if your children become associated with some religious group and it results in their becoming more withdrawn, silent, hostile, angry, or their newfound faith results in extreme, bizarre behavior or unconventional styles of dress, they need help! Christianity does not require that.

According to the Apostle Paul, "What does it matter if you can speak in tongues? If you don't have love, it's not worth anything! And what does it matter if you can do miraculous things? Without love, it's all empty and worthless! And what does it matter if you can quote reams of scripture and spout high-sounding theology into the air! Without love, it's only so much noise! Faith, hope, love abide, these three; but the greatest of these is love." (1 Corinthians 13:8-13, paraphrase) So, put love first and make love your aim. That's what God wants you to do.

The fourth quality of good religion is that it will keep you connected to God's people, to His church. It's a good idea to stay close to the mainline churches — churches that have stood the test of time and which, through thick and thin, good times and bad, have proven themselves worthy of your trust. Be very careful of the fly-by-night religious personalities who zip into town with an easy one-step program to salvation, or twelve-step program to personal recovery and restoration, or a few exotic gimmicks, then just as quickly zip away, never to be seen again. Beware of those who try to steal you away from your church with smooth talk and pious smiles and cloaked innuendoes which suggest, ever so subtly, that the church you are now in just isn't as spiritual as they are. Be careful of organizations which use religious vocabulary and even quote scripture to motivate you to sell their products, make them a profit, and at the same time, satisfy your own greed and lust for money and material possessions. Bad religion says, "What's in it for me?" Good religion says, "What can I do for God and for his church? He loved it and gave himself for it. What can I do —what can I give – for His church?

Jesus warned us to watch out for wolves in sheep's clothing. They make so much sense sometimes. They appeal to dome of our basic needs and promise to make even our most ambitious dreams come true. They look so genuine. The fact is: we **want** them to be real.

But if you really don't know – if you're bewildered about the difference between good and bad religion – bring it all to Jesus. He is our pattern, our blueprint, our measuring stick. For Christians, He is the **real test** of good religion, authentic faith, and genuine spirituality. Ultimately, our eternal destiny will be determined by whether He knows us.

If you come, you can be introduced to Him today!

IT LOOKS LIKE IT'S GONNA' RAIN
Matthew 7:24-27

SEVERAL YEARS AGO, A GROUP OF West Texas Jaycees decided to reconstruct the notorious, wild west town called Boot Hill as a tourist attraction. Early in the process, they uncovered the old cowboy cemetery with a great many of the old tombstones still intact. Volunteers immediately cleaned it up and restored it to its original condition.

One of the tombstones in the middle of the cemetery captured the most attention. It bore no name or date, only four simple lines. The epitaph read:

> Here lies a man...name unknown
> Mourned in no one's prayers,
> Where he's gone, no one knows,
> And no one really cares.

It's tragic to realize that that's all that's left of someone's life. Whoever he was, he was given the wonderful gift of life, along with an opportunity to do something with it –to leave something behind. All he left, however, was a public notice that no one had cared while he lived and no one cared that he was gone. I can't help but wonder what he had set out to do with his life and where, along the way, he went wrong. Did he ever realize the mistakes that he had made and did he ever make any attempt to turn around his life?

Jesus wrapped up his Sermon on the Mount with the story of two men who started out with very clear notions of what they wanted out of life. It's one of the simplest stories Jesus ever told. In fact, the truth it tells is so plain and important that it's one of the first of Jesus' parables that we teach out children.

It's about two men who are alike in so many ways. They are both interested in, want, and work very hard for the same thing. What's more, each one could have what he dreamed of without having to compete against or deprive the other. In fact, what they want is what we all want - just to build a comfortable life where they could live out their days in relative happiness with their family and friends. If we accomplish that, most of us would feel like we have it "made."

What's interesting about life, though, is that even when we want the same thing, we often go after it in such different ways. Take the two men in this story, for example. Luke's version indicates that "the wise man dug deep and laid the foundation on the rock." (Luke 6:48) Apparently, his greatest desire was to build something which would last – perhaps, even the house in which he planned to retire. Sp, he didn't mind putting in the extra effort such an undertaking required.

Luke recalls that the other man – the one Jesus called a fool –built his house upon the ground without a foundation. (v.29) What he built was more like a playhouse than a permanent dwelling. He was in more of a hurry. Foolish folks almost always are, aren't they? They have no time to wait. They seem to always want what they want right now. Hardly ever do they take the time to dig a foundation. They take every shortcut they can find. Every way to cut corners in order to save a little time and a few dollars is OK with them.

When a fool builds a house, he seldom thinks all the way through. He never stops to consider the possibilities or envision the eventualities. He never stops to ask: "Now, what will happen when the snow thaws and the spring rains begin? Will this petty little trout stream suddenly overflow its banks and flood me out? So, one of the things this story is about is taking the time to think things through, putting in the extra effort to dig a little deeper in order to lay a solid foundation.

It's obvious what Jesus is telling us. He's urging us to prepare the houses we're building – the lives we're living – for wind, rain and flood. If we expect to stand, to last, and to endure, we can't build just for fair weather, calm winds, and bright skies. Rather, we must build with a view to the hours of crisis because eventually, the storms break over us all. Everyone gets a turn at weathering high winds.

You are not the only one who has found life hard. There's a story about a man who went through the great flood of the Ohio Valley in the 1930s. It was a tragic and devastating experience and he just couldn't get over it. He talked about his unfortunate experience constantly. When he died and went to heaven, Saint Peter asked him if there was anything he would especially like to do. The man replied that he would like Peter to get together a crowd so that he could tell them about his horrible experiences on the Ohio Valley flood. Peter immediately called together a crowd of a million persons. The man was overjoyed. He had never had that kind of audience before. Just as the man started to tell his sad tale, however, Peter told him, "Oh, there's just one thing you might like to know. Brother Noah is in the audience."

Sometimes it's easy to think we're the only ones who have ever experienced the storms of life. Sometimes, we even act as if it's only the good people like us who go through hard times. But everyone gets a turn. Bad things don't just happen to good people. It's just that good people sometimes think they've earned an exemption.

Jesus never tells us where we can build a house where there are no storms. This story is not about our safe haven in which we can build a home, grow a family, and raise our children, Shangri-La simply doesn't exist! Jesus made it very clear that every house we build must be able to endure less-than-an-ideal climate.

Jesus loves us too much to be anything but brutally honest. He thought we ought to know that it looks like it's gonna' rain at some point in our life. He thought that it would help us to know that while we're still working on the foundation. Unfortunately, not enough of us are willing to listen. Not enough of us are building lives which will endure the storms. In a frantic rush to live higher than we should – much beyond our means – to cultivate the right friends, move in the right circles, achieve the highest measure of success, we have failed to lay the proper foundation. At the first sting of pain or unexpected shift in plans, our lives too often collapse like a house of cards. The story tells us the truth: if we build on sand – no matter how many degrees we hold, no matter how high we've climbed, how far we have gone – if God is not under us as the foundation of life, we simply have that much farther to fall.

You may get along for a number of years. But one year the snow will be unusually heavy. There'll be a quick thaw in the Spring and on top of that, the heavy rains will come. Then, the character of what you've built will be put to the test. It may have happened to you already. The storms may have already take their toll – they've broken some of you- and you've discovered that you've been putting some pretty shoddy stuff into the life you're building- stuff which will never stand the test of the storm.

A casual observer may not even notice that you're having a particularly difficult time. The difference in the way people build their lives is not always apparent. People, marriages, families, often look very much alike. It's pretty hard sometimes to tell which is built on a solid foundation and which is not.

It's even difficult to tell with Christians. Apparently, the two people Jesus contrasted in this parable were disciples. They both heard his word. Maybe they attended the same church, sat on the same pew, listened to the same sermons, read the same version of scripture, loved the same hymns, and enjoyed the fellowship of mutual Christian friends. But the issue Jesus raised is not merely whether they **hear** the word of God, but whether they **do something** about what they hear! **That** is what determines the nature of life's foundation.

Sometimes, it's not just the wind and the rain and the floods you have to worry about. Sometimes, the earthquake comes and the earth begins to literally move under your feet. Sometimes, the foundations even begin to shake. Earthquake specialists have discovered that corner reinforcements which extend the side walls of a house and attach it to the foundation greatly strengthen the house against horizontal land movement. In an earthquake, non-bolted houses move a few inches from its foundation and structures collapse. A safe house, on the other hand, is one that relates as much as possible to its foundation. It not only rests upon a rock. It is built upon the rock.

Jesus said that the only secure foundation- the only life that will withstand the wind and rain, flood and earthquake – is the life grounded in His word. That grounding means more than merely hearing it or knowing it. Being grounded in His word means doing it, living by it. It means to be obedient even when, humanly speaking, it seems foolish to be obedient.

To obey His word means to do it all. He doesn't give us the option of picking and choosing those parts of His word we prefer – the bits and pieces which we perceive will make our life easier or our careers more successful. It means that we obey it- even when we're not certain about all that it entails, nor even what the consequences of our obedience might be.

Mark Twain, one of the sturdiest of all skeptics about things spiritual, once confessed that what bothered him most about the Bible was not the parts that he did not understand. What gave him the most trouble were the parts he understood completely. I think I know what he meant, don't you?

The story is not calling on us to merely **do something – that is, do anything**. Jesus is calling on us to the right kind of action. The fool's trouble was not that he failed to act, but that he did the wrong thing. He built a life. He just went about it all wrong. He built it on the wrong foundation!

No matter how feverishly, diligently, and sincerely you have fashioned your life –no matter how fastidious you have been to give it the right "look", the most appealing appearance – no matter how much you may have sacrificed in order to get where you are – unless it has been built upon **the** foundation, "great will be the fall of it." One day the storms will blow against it and tear it all down!"

There is nothing you can do to keep the storms away. Likewise, there is nothing else you can do to stand strong in the storms than to dig your foundations deep in Jesus. The Apostle Paul reminds us that that "...God has...placed Jesus Christ as the one and only foundation, and no other foundation can be laid. (1 Corinthians 3:11)

Some of you are in the midst of the storms right now. You never knew that life could be so frustrating, frightening, and confusing. You always thought your marriage was strong, your family secure. The two of you have been through so much together. But lately, things have begun to change. You've lost interest. You just don't care as much as you once cared.

Mid-life crisis was something everyone else went through, not you! But there are times when you'd give almost anything to be free of all responsibilities and obligations.

Suddenly, you've become afraid of dying – of coming down with cancer or some other debilitating, painful illness. Or, you're afraid of growing old – of being left alone- of being placed in a nursing home.

You're out of work – or afraid that you're going to be. You worry about losing everything. You wonder where God is and why he doesn't do something.

The storms have broken over you and frankly, you aren't weathering it very well right now. In fact, you really feel quite shaky. You aren't sure how long you can hold on. Your friends and family – those who genuinely care about you – tell you to stick it out, to wait. Things will eventually get better.

Recently, one of our teachers told me about going into her class one morning and finding a little first grade boy standing up in front of the class with his stomach stuck way out. Thinking that was a rather odd thing to do, she asked him, "Why are you standing there with your stomach sticking out?"

"Well," the little boy responded. "I had a tummy ache this morning and I went to the nurse. She said, "Just stick it out until noon and maybe it'll be OK.'"

Some people go through life like that – just sticking it out until noon, hoping things will get better. But life is more than "just sticking it out." It's a wonderful gift – even with all its stresses and problems, its pressures and storms. God wants our life to be full, meaningful, abundant, and enduring.

There is life in the storms and through the storms, and even after the storms. And that's what this story is all about. There is no storm that is so powerful – no wind that is so frightening- that God is not able to withstand it. And as long as your life is linked to His, you too will be able to endure!

Do you remember the words of the old gospel hymn, "The Solid Rock"?

When darkness seems to hide His face,
I rest on His unchanging grace;

In every high and stormy gale,
My anchor holds within the veil.

On Christ, the Sold Rock, I stand,
All other ground is sinking sand!

It looks like it's gonna' rain. You may not be able to see the clouds now, but they're building. You may not believe me. But it's true. One day, there'll be a downpour. Will your life stand up when the storms come?

www.ingramcontent.com/pod-product-compliance
Lightning Source LLC
Chambersburg PA
CBHW031258090426
42742CB00007B/502